9.95

DATE DUE

APR 26 1999			

21,006

Total Tennis

THE MIND-BODY METHOD

M. Barrie Richmond, M.D.

In Collaboration with Jane Carley

Preface by John Newcombe

MACMILLAN PUBLISHING CO., INC.

NEW YORK

Macmillan Publishing Co., Inc.
866 Third Avenue, New York, N.Y. 10022
Collier Macmillan Canada, Ltd.

Library of Congress Cataloging in Publication Data
Richmond, M   Barrie.
   Total tennis.
   Includes index.
   1. Tennis—Psychological aspects. I. Carley, Jane, joint author. II. Title.
GV1002.9.P75R52   796.34'2'01   79-24704
ISBN 0-02-603180-9

First Printing 1980
Printed in the United States of America

Photo of Chris Evert Lloyd by Melchior DiGiacomo. All other photos courtesy of *Tennis Week*.

For my wife,
Lois Barrett Richmond,
and our three sons, Joshua,
Aryeh, and Noah

Contents

Preface

Tennis has come a long way in the twelve years since the advent of open tennis. One of the biggest changes has been the influence the top players have had on teaching methods and how the game should be played. Evert Lloyd, Connors, and Borg gave authenticity to the two-handed backhand. Nastase, Vilas, and a host of others proved that there is no *one* way to play the game. There are, of course, certain boundaries to stay within, but today's top pros have shown that there are many different ways of approaching and finishing the various strokes. In the fifties, when I learned to play tennis, the grips and strokes were taught along strict, accepted lines.

Many tennis books were published in the seventies offering new ideas and ways for the club player to learn the game. *Inner Tennis*, one of the leading tennis how-to books, emphasized the mental side of learning. I have never believed that tennis, or any sport, can be that simple. There is a physical side that is just as important as relaxing mentally and enjoying the sport. I feel that to be good at any sport, it must be appreciated and practiced. The combination of the mental and physical is called practical teaching. This is the approach used at our tennis resorts and the one I've used to develop my game.

M. Barrie Richmond explains the practical approach to tennis better than anyone I've read before and calls it "total tennis." He correctly points out that the right mental approach, while being extremely important, is of no value unless you're able to reach the ball and play your shot.

In *Total Tennis* the homework has been done. Richmond's remarks about top players and their weaknesses and strengths are right on target. The early chapter on choking really gets into the problem with some of the best anecdotes I have ever read or heard.

By reading this book closely, you will not only improve your tennis game, but you will also learn a great deal about your own personal weaknesses and strengths.

I congratulate Barrie on a well-written and well-thought-out book about tennis. You'll find no gimmicks in these pages. Follow his advice and there's no way you won't improve your game and overall approach to the sport.

—JOHN NEWCOMBE

Acknowledgments

I am grateful to Jane Carley for her extraordinary skill and commitment in guiding me through every facet of the organization and writing of this book.

I am indebted to several psychoanalytic colleagues whose ideas and insights I have applied in building the thesis of this book. Dr. Haskell E. Bernstein's penetrating insights into the psychology of self-esteem and tension regulation have furthered my understanding of the emotions experienced by tennis players. Dr. Fred P. Robbins's conceptualizations of psychological change in learning and mastery have helped me in developing the problem-solution perspective of this book. And Dr. Robert Koff made valuable suggestions that I have incorporated into the "Learning" chapter.

Four outstanding U.S. Professional Tennis Association teaching pros have taught me a great deal about the practical and aesthetic aspects of tennis. Ray Baladad's discussions with me about teaching and coaching tennis were a crucial stimulus for this book. Drew Bracken, Corky Leighton, and Tolly Riaz have also shared with me their understanding of the learning and mastery of tennis. My appreciative thanks to Macmillan editor Jeanne Fredericks for her encouragement and sound editorial advice.

Finally, I want to thank two tennis-playing friends, Sue and Bob Wieseneck, for their suggestions and advice on portions of the preliminary manuscript.

Total Tennis

Introduction

Tennis is a mind-body game. To play it well, your mind and body must work together. When the mind-body unit is working in harmony, strokes and footwork are coordinated, concentration is uninterrupted, and one good shot reinforces the next. This makes for Total Tennis.

How is it done? This book will show you how to play a consistently good—even excellent—game. The key is understanding how emotion, intellect, and body interact in achieving mastery. We call it Total Tennis because it takes into account all the physical and mental factors that influence your play. More than anything, Total Tennis is a viewpoint—one that can change your entire court performance.

To facilitate the integration of emotion, intellect, and body, it is necessary to understand in depth the potential of the body and mind to function as a cohesive unit. Understanding mind-body interaction will enable you to work out inner tensions, establish a confident attitude, and deal effectively with the challenges you face on the court.

Whether you are a beginner or a tournament player, unforced errors on the tennis court are ultimately traceable to a *dys*-integration of mind and body. To solve your problems, it's absolutely vital to achieve mind-body integration. Sometimes it's not easy for the player to pinpoint a problem because so much is going on all at once: the body must make use of past practice, conditioning, and drills, to perform specific coordinated functions almost automatically; the mind must react to unpredictable situations and make strategic on-the-spot decisions.

But perfectly coordinated functioning is, of course, an ideal rarely achieved. The body tells us when everything isn't working together by faltering when we get emotionally tense. This is called *choking*. It happens when, despite all ef-

3

forts, the player's body *will not* do what it *can* do, because something interrupts the mind-body unity. An anxious player may find it impossible to stay down and follow through on his backhand return of serve, even though hours of drill may have been spent on it. A perfectionist may become nervous and make unrealistic demands on his body, attempting near-impossible shots or placements. He may start worrying about his effectiveness or wondering whether he is going to win, and suddenly his timing goes down the drain.* Every tennis player has experienced choking; in competition we all tend to lose our cool. What can we do about it?

Understanding potential interferences with mind-body integration is the first step to an effective and sustained mind-body synthesis. Using both your intellect (in strategy) and your body (in conditioning and drills) is necessary to develop and perfect your tennis game. Total Tennis goes a crucial step further, linking intellect and body training with the emotional awareness that can activate your tennis performance.

Emotions play a tremendous role in tennis. Self-assertiveness, confidence, and the desire for mastery—and their opposites, timidity, poor self-esteem, and the fear of success—constantly affect the player's form and style. They can constitute positive or negative motivations, and thus have a profound influence on how the player learns and performs. Total Tennis will lead you to an awareness of your hidden feelings and psychological motivations so that you can understand and improve your mind-body interaction on the court. Total Tennis proposes a solid, down-to-earth understanding of how to improve your play by learning about your motives. In applying basic psychological insights to performance problems, we systematically take up the practical problems of the tennis player at different ages and stages of ability.

Mastery is the name of the game. And it takes work, both

---

* For the sake of grammatical expediency, we will use masculine pronouns to generalize about both sexes, even though this convention often suggests a male image when a female image would be equally appropriate.

physical and mental. Correct stroke production in tennis is complex, and "what comes naturally" is sometimes wrong. Physical practice, self-understanding, motivation, and the ability to regulate psychological tensions are the essential factors in achieving mastery. Tennis strokes are far too complex to be learned as single holistic units, nor can any stroke be totally mastered. This book links the practical with the theoretical in a way that utilizes the best of the intuitive and checkpoint learning methods in tennis.

Tennis improvement is significantly influenced by the teaching professional, who must not only evaluate the talent and emotional commitment of his student, but also understand how the student learns and how he manages his feelings in competitive play. A dynamic learning alliance between student and teacher arises naturally when they both understand the motives and tensions involved in learning. This book will help both student and teacher to achieve the collaboration necessary for true integrative learning, through a thorough understanding of how the mind works with—and against—the body. Timothy Gallwey, author of *The Inner Game of Tennis,* rightly emphasizes that the best learning takes place when the student is *aware* of what is happening; that experiencing exactly *where the racquet is* is much better than mechanically trying to imitate someone else's stroke. Yet we *can* learn by imitation and by drill. The essential task is to pull together our perceptions, body memories, and inner psychological experiences so that positive, integrative learning occurs.

The mind-body perspective is especially helpful for children who want to learn and master the game. Children's tennis presents extraordinary opportunities for emotional and physical development, but brings with it potential problems. A child's motivation in playing tennis is different from an adult's; children are easily influenced by parents, friends, tennis teachers, and coaches. Carefully assessing the child's needs and capabilities can help avert pitfalls—due to lack of talent, resources, time, or parental support—in the child's tennis-learning experience. Problems can arise, too, when parents or coaches try to push children to success. This book will help you smooth the way over these possible rough spots, and will deal with such questions as "When is the best time to start lessons?" "How soon should a child enter school or tournament competitions?" and "How should a talented junior be stimulated?" As in the rest of the book, the emphasis is on integrative learning.

A series of psychological profiles of some outstanding tennis champions—Billie Jean King, Bjorn Borg, Chris Evert Lloyd, Jimmy Connors, Tracy Austin, Ilie Nastase, Martina Navratilova, Guillermo Vilas, Evonne Goolagong, and John McEnroe—forms the final chapter. Their different personalities and styles on the court illustrate how they handle the intrapsychic tensions stimulated by competitive play. The winning streaks, slumps, and fascinating interpersonal rivalries of these champions reflect their natural abilities and styles of dealing with their aggressive and narcissistic tensions. These champions' strengths and weaknesses are analyzed to show how their self-mastery leads them to the highest levels of mind-body integration.

Lessons, practices, and drills, as well as conditioning programs, are necessary for improving your game. But to profit from physical work, you must find out what happens to your emotions when you are on the court. Psychological terms such as *narcissism, tension regulation,* and *competitive conflicts* will be used in this book. Some explanation of these psychological concepts will help you understand what's behind your tennis game.

Narcissism

In modern psychological usage, the term *narcissism* refers to a healthy self-interest. It's normal to want for yourself and to be concerned about yourself, but if a person has excessive self-interest or is afraid to show any self-interest, his narcissism is considered "pathological," interfering with his capacity to cope realistically with life.

We all know people who are excessively self-involved or

grandiose about themselves. We also know people who constantly put themselves down and overidealize others. These are narcissistic problems that can interfere with mind-body integration; undervaluing yourself or your opponent will get you into trouble on the court. The closer you are to narcissistic balance, the better your game will be.

The pathologically narcissistic person needs to underrate or overvalue himself in order to achieve psychological balance; he needs to see others as either better or lesser than himself because it's the only way he can feel good about himself. The out-of-balance, narcissistic tennis player is easily bored, often impatient or temperamental, and suffers considerable depression when he loses. He rarely feels "together" and may feel hopeless about improving his court performance.

Narcissistic conflicts, however, can sometimes help to further mind-body integration. If a player is grandiose, his fantasies of winning may sustain him and even push him on to victories. If he underrates himself, he may find the challenge stimulating when he faces an overrated opponent. In general, then, normal narcissistic feelings add zest to a game, but a player who bases his performance on narcissistic needs cannot consistently hold his game together.

Perfectionism is a narcissistic trait. Since the pathologically narcissistic player operates from a feeling of defectiveness or deficiency, he usually has to choose between two extremes: either give up, or become excessively perfectionistic to compensate for his inner feeling of inferiority. The narcissistic perfectionist *hates* to play unless he plays well, and therefore tends to fuss more about who he plays with, where and when they play, the condition of the court, and the weather. If he makes a bad shot, he takes it hard and may punish himself by feeling terrible about not having practiced enough. He has too much emotion invested in playing well, and his need to be perfect interferes with his functioning.

The player who overrates his abilities has a narcissistic problem too, despite his show of self-confidence. He may compensate for his feelings of inadequacy by displaying an artificial enthusiasm on the court, constantly bragging about his good shots and forgetting about his unforced errors or blaming them on court conditions. Like the perfectionist who berates himself for his errors, the grandiose show-off player with unresolved narcissistic conflicts is prone to inconsistent performance. The show-off may play brilliantly at times, but his performance depends too much on external factors such as a coach's encouragement, audience support, or favorable line calls. Tennis is more than a game for him—it's a means of achieving the psychological balance he lacks. And since psychological balance is a prerequisite to a good tennis game, the overly narcissistic player is always one step behind.

You may have realized by now that the distinction between pathological and normal narcissism is a matter of degree. Even the well-integrated, even-tempered player will occasionally experience some narcissistic tension that interferes with his play. The finest athlete may experience a narcissistic breakdown that leads to sudden choking or to a prolonged, depressing slump.

Tension Regulation

Everyone, even the calmest person, has emotional tensions. Psychologically speaking, tension is the pressure to act; what you do about the pressure can be described as your mode of tension regulation. Each person has an individualized way of regulating tensions, and it shows up on the court. A woman may push her stroke because she doesn't trust herself to make a full, coordinated stroke that requires a backswing and follow-through. The player who looks up too quickly and fails to hit through also has a problem in tension regulation. The player who performs well is motivated by many tensions, but has developed a good style of regulating them so that they do not interfere with function.

Tension regulation is closely linked to mind-body integration. Without it there is no consistent coordination, and the player often resorts to impulsive action to compensate for his loss of control. This signals a breakdown in tension regulation. When does tension regulation break down? Mostly when a player experiences an unexpected tension (pressure to act) arising from a strong conflictual emotion. Getting in touch with conflictual emotions, and understanding their impact on performance, will help you to deal with them.

Aggressive and Competitive Conflicts

Tennis is a superb medium for the expression of aggressive tensions. It allows us to attack, express hostility, and conquer, all within a friendly, civilized framework. Although aggression is a natural human drive, we are taught early in life that we must not show hostility, and we learn to repress aggressive feelings.

Aggression and latent hatreds often get pushed down so far into the unconscious mind that it becomes difficult to step onto the tennis court and release the *appropriate* aggressive feelings. This is where conflict comes in. Some players find it difficult to be aggressive enough, because they are unconsciously afraid of losing control of the deep hostilities they have repressed since childhood. Or they may lack experience in being aggressive because they are not used to situations that demand the expression of competitive or hostile impulses. Other players may be able to express their aggressive feelings, but get so tripped up by the intensity of these feelings that their mind-body integration is destroyed.

Good tennis playing requires the expression of aggressions, but this does not mean that you should learn to hurl the tennis racquet at your opponent's head when you get annoyed. The *mode* of expression can vary from a low growl to a well-executed overhead smash; the important thing is that you become aware of your aggressive tensions and release them in a way that helps you feel good and play well.

In situations of great pressure or intense feeling, repressed aggression may break through unexpectedly. This can be a startling experience, since deep aggressive feelings often have a primitive quality running counter to the aesthetic values of court etiquette. A woman I know was shocked by her hostile feelings when, after four years of gentle, nonaggressive playing, she began to feel a hostile energy on the court, and in moments of intense play noticed herself thinking, "I'll *murder* you!" When she stopped feeling shock at the intensity of her feelings, she was able to release them in powerful strokes and aggressive strategies that improved her game greatly.

Much of mind-body integration lies in the ability to face aggressive feelings and channel tensions into a positive, natural tennis style. That style will be different for each player, because everyone has different aggressive conflicts and different degrees of repression. Part of Total Tennis is finding out about yourself and your aggressive feelings so that you can regulate your tensions and function smoothly on the court.

·1·

Choking

What is choking? *Webster's* defines it as the inability to function efficiently in a critical situation because of tenseness. Tennis players know that no dictionary definition of the choke can convey the frustration experienced when they lose control of the direction of their game. They lose their touch, stop thinking, freeze, or tighten up; it happens to everyone, beginner or pro, at one time or another.

Choking is essentially a failure of mind-body integration. It can show up in a sudden loss of speed, stamina, coordination, or timing that can cause you to miss the easiest setup. Or it may appear in a more subtle undermining of effectiveness, so that even though you seem to be doing everything right, nothing works. Whatever form choking takes, it is always a matter of the player being unable to perform to his capability. Choking comes on inexplicably, hangs on with a vengeance, and almost seems like an external condition affecting the player's performance. Sometimes victims of choking blame court conditions or "bad luck." This kind of rationalizing may temporarily ease the pain of losing, but it won't improve anyone's game. The real cause of choking is inside the player. If you want to combat choking and improve your game, you must find out what's causing *your* choking, face up to it, and work through it until your mind and body are functioning together at top capacity.

First of all, it's important to deal with excuses and rationalizations. It's true that gusting winds, poor lighting, or a closely contested tournament match may wreak havoc on your performance, but you'll notice that such factors don't always interfere with your play; some people even play better under external pressures. This is because the external pressure is only the secondary cause of choking. Whether the external pressure causes you to choke depends on whether it evokes deeper psychological tensions in you.

You're not a tense player? Think about it. People who are highly motivated to be effective (and that includes most tennis players, especially those who picked up this book) often won't even admit to themselves that they are tense. They work around their tensions, control their feelings, and become masters at smoothing over the raw, aggressive feelings that are naturally excited on the court. They don't throw tantrums, they don't seethe at a close line call. They're so much in control that they are *not aware* of the anxieties that may be stirred up inside, the tension that can take hold of the hand that grips the racquet that sends the ball straight into the net. But that tension is always there.

How can you become aware of your tensions? Whenever you play poorly, observe your feelings after the game. See how often you end up justifying your losses. Examine the external pressures that you blame, and look for the feelings that were evoked by them during the game. These feelings will be connected to the deep-seated tensions that interfere with optimal coordinated functioning. They are the hidden tensions, the unexpressed tensions that choke your play. As a simple example, imagine two players, A and B, reacting to close line calls: player A becomes infuriated and demands that the call be reversed; player B smiles good-humoredly and plays the next point with calm control. Both players may be equally enraged, but one of them is *expressing* his rage and the other is *suppressing* it. Neither will improve his game. Explosive player A acts to offend others and will simply continue to exhibit his tensions without being aware of their deeper meaning; player B's main concern is self-control, and he succeeds only in defending himself from facing the reality of the aggressive tensions behind his calm behavior. Keeping your cool on the court has to be an in-depth experience rather than a superficial suppression of tensions.

Where are those tensions hidden? In our conscious mind we are simply playing a game of tennis. We may be aware of aggressive, competitive feelings, but we are not aware of the fact that in our unconscious mind we are using every element of the game symbolically in order to fulfill deep psychological needs. When things go well, normal needs for attaining perfection and complete control are experienced consciously in a pleasurable sense of mastery. When things go badly, unpredictable anxieties are evoked in us, and without time to think about what's happening, our unconscious mind leaps back to every pressure experienced since early childhood. Panic! You're out of commission. Choke.

It's hard to locate these unconscious feelings. But since they are the root cause of your choking, look for clues. If you've made a series of unforced errors, look back to what happened earlier in the game to see if you can find something that may have stirred up tensions you were unaware of. If you find that you choked soon after a close line call, chances are that you suppressed your reaction to that call, and those inhibited tensions were rechanneled, adversely affecting your mobility, balance, weight transfer, or stroke production. Further introspection will help you to understand how the unforced errors were linked to the close line call; you may notice that after the call you became distracted or experienced a change in your timing. Why? Because the call evoked specific, intense feelings that you could not handle satisfactorily and therefore suppressed. Whenever you sense your concentration is beginning to fail, or you are becoming too easily distracted, consider the possibility that some internal tension has been evoked, then suppressed, and has interfered with your mind-body integration.

One tennis pro noticed that in tournament competition he played extremely well against inferior opponents, whereas in close matches he tightened up—he'd be half a step slower at the net and sometimes sluggish on crucial points. When a junior player told him, "In practice you're great, but in a tough match you're slow as molasses," he linked his mobility problem to the pressure of facing difficult opponents. He admitted that at first he was stunned because he had not noticed in himself what he was so quick to observe in others— the tell-tale clues that signal the failures of mind-body integration on the court. Once he realized the significance of the junior player's observation, he did some serious introspection. He gradually realized that several deep feelings were involved, and he described his choking experience this way:

> I'm afraid to fail. I'm afraid to *try* and then fail. If I'm not immediately superior to my opponent, I tend to get discouraged. Rather than appear a weaker person, I give up. Physically, I move slower. Obviously my play gets worse as a result. I suffer from a real lack of concentration, experience intense anxiety and even self-pity when I can't perform automatically. Before I know it, I find myself longing to get the match over with, to get off the court.

This player is close to dealing with his choking problem because he has identified the issues that lead to his choking: preoccupation with superiority/inferiority; fear of humiliation if he loses; and the inability to stay with the battle once these feelings are aroused.

These problems are different for everyone. Here's another example of a player trying to identify her choking problem:

> My game has simply fallen apart. I feel intimidated by my opponent, especially if she makes hostile remarks or seems in any way to be putting me down. Sometimes I won't make a line call, even if her shot is clearly out, because I don't want to stir up a fuss. Later I feel enraged with myself for giving away crucial points. But at the time it's never clear to me what I should do. My playing obviously suffers—I get distracted, and instead of concentrating on the next point I find myself obsessed with what happened before.

Though it may look simple, it takes some hard thinking to arrive at a precise, objective self-diagnosis like this one. Most people don't get this far. This player is aware that her choking stems from the feeling that her opponent is putting her down. She may *know* it's not true, but she still has that *feeling*, and it ruins her mind-body integration. She needs to study that feeling whenever it comes up (undoubtedly she has it off the court too) and to find out where it comes from. She also needs to distinguish between assertive action and hostile aggression.

If an opponent's shot is out, it is not a hostile act to say so—it's the appropriate assertive action. It can be learned and used once the player has worked on his feelings of intimidation. If you don't have the feeling that your opponent is out to get you personally then you can feel comfortable about challenging him and beating him. When you feel comfortable, your choking will diminish.

You will never feel comfortable on the court unless you can identify the feelings causing you to choke. And you may have a delayed reaction in even *feeling* those feelings if the situation is complex or ambiguous. A friend of mine once described to me this common problem from doubles play:

> I called "fault" on a close first serve to my partner that was an inch out. I glanced at my opponent at the net, and he was smirking. I just went on playing. The next serve, as luck would have it, was also out, but I didn't call it—it all happened so fast. My partner netted the ball and lost the point. Then the server hit a wide-angled serve that caught me off balance, and I netted the ball. At that moment I realized that I should have called the second close serve, and I started getting distracted. They kept the momentum, and we lost.
>
> That night I was so infuriated with myself, I couldn't sleep. Why hadn't I called the second serve? Giving him that call had been the turning point; after that I couldn't recover my concentration. Finally I realized that I hadn't called the second serve because I had felt intimidated by my opponent's smirking at my first call! But if I had felt like that, why hadn't I challenged him?

This kind of problem is complex and not easily worked out. The player first had to clarify what the sequence of events was, and then determine how those events had influenced his play. To understand that his problem was with assertive action, he had to realize that the smirk had had a more devastating effect than he had first wanted to acknowledge. After thinking it through, he resolved that in the future, whenever an opponent did something that affected his equilibrium, he would be more aware of his own reactions, rather than suppress them and end up befuddled. By following through on his resolution, and adding to it months of court experience and analytic hindsight, he was able to get closer to his feelings on the court and channel them into appropriate, on-the-spot actions that eliminated his assertive-action choking. He trained himself to stop play whenever he felt his opponents were questioning his calls. In doubles matches, if his net opponent gestured or indicated doubt about a close serve, he routinely stopped play and asked, "Do you have some question about my call?" In this way he learned to deal with the tensions that previously had always interrupted his concentration. He expanded his techniques for assertive action, as I noticed when I watched him play recently:

> In a close match, with the score tied at 3-3 in the third set, he hit a cross-court forehand just out of his opponent's reach and scored an outright winner. But his opponent kept staring at the spot where the ball had landed, as if to say, "Damn it, that ball was so close, I can't call it out, but I'm not sure it was in either." My friend reacted at once by asking, "Did you see it out?" (He was remembering Vic Braden's TV tip that unless your opponent is sure the ball is out, the point continues.) The opponent agreed that he hadn't seen it out. That ended that.

Once you catch on to the idea of assertive action and link it with your emotional tensions, your concentration won't be affected by on-the-court distractions. My friend's method for on-the-spot self-assertion may or may not be the best solution for you. But with experience and reflection, you can develop your own techniques to deal with close line calls, your opponent's delays, and the thousand distractions that come up in social and competitive tennis. As you work on your methods for dealing with sticky on-the-court tensions, keep a vigilant eye on how you react when your emotional equilibrium is disturbed. The natural tendency is to put these feelings aside because it's hard to know what to do when they arise. But if you acknowledge your emotions and your tendency to suppress them, then you can work toward effective solutions.

The conflictual feelings behind choking usually lie in more than one area, which is another reason why they're so hard to identify. What may seem like a problem with assertive action may actually be a different problem. Recently a frustrated pro complained:

> My opponent was a player who is notorious for giving bad calls. He even resorts to racial slurs to throw his opponents off balance. I went in determined not to let him get to me, but two close calls cost me the one service break he needed to win the first set 6-3, and I was fuming. So when he started losing in the second set and called my return of serve—a clear winner—out and at 15-30, I jumped over the net and went after him. He wouldn't change his call. By that time I was so furious that I hit his second serve at 30-30 into the stands; it should have been 15-40. I couldn't stand it, so I just walked off the court.

Why didn't this player assert himself by getting a linesman for the bad calls? He had often advised junior players to insist on having a linesman if bad calls became a problem. "I don't know," he said. "I guess I felt I could beat him no matter what he pulled, because I was the better player. I felt as if getting a linesman would be making an excuse for my losing. I was more enraged with myself than with him."

This pro was letting his feelings of superiority get in the way. He was handicapping himself to prove his superiority. It was unnecessary and it worked against him. Never let your feelings about the quality of your play interfere with your judgment. If you really feel good about how you play, you won't want to play against unfair odds.

Choking is always a signal of suppressed tensions seeking expression. These tensions are rooted in childhood experiences, mainly in the socializing process during which each child gradually learns that certain feelings such as anger, selfishness, and envy should not be expressed. To avoid shame and embarrassment, the child learns either to supress the "dangerous" feeling or to channel its expression into acceptable forms of behavior. (Tennis itself is an outlet for suppressed aggressive tensions.) It follows that if you can find out what emotions were evoked and suppressed before a sudden fall in performance, you will have a good line on your choking problem.

Identifying a subtle problem in self-confidence can lead to a significant change in your results. Brian Gottfried described the turning point in his singles career as having occurred in a match he played against Bjorn Borg at Forest Hills in the 1976 U.S. Open. Gottfried, usually a slow starter, won the first two sets, and was leading 2-0 in the third. At 30-30 he double-faulted. Borg won the next point to break serve, and Gottfried was able to win only eight more games in the last three sets. Human failure? Borg's grim coolness? Gottfried said:

> It was ridiculous. Here I was, up two sets and a break, four games from the match, and *I honestly didn't think I could win*. Whenever I'd get in a big match like this one, I just played to make it close. But losing that time had a big effect on me. Never again have I gone in against anybody thinking I couldn't win.[1]

Gottfried's emotional tensions had surfaced on the court as he was losing, and he realized that winning and losing are things that happen inside the player's mind. "Suddenly it clicked inside," he said:

> Usually after a tough five-setter like that I'd be upset. But I remember it *not* bothering me. I think it hit me that there I'd been, in the fourth round of the Open, in the stadium, against the number one player in the world. I said, "If I can play that way all the time and just believe in myself a little more." Looking back, I must have been thinking about what would happen if I won instead of about closing out the match. Now, when I get behind, I feel I can come back. A guy's serving for the set, yet I feel if I play it right, it's not over. I will come back. And when I'm ahead, I think only of staying there. What it comes down to is, I'm not beating myself by overthinking or by intimidating myself or being intimidated. If I lose now, it'll be because the guy was too good that day.[2]

By observing his paradoxical reaction—that he hadn't been upset after losing a tough five-set match—it dawned on Gottfried that despite numerous successes, he still had not resolved a lack of confidence in himself. The fact that Borg was number one had intimidated him. His analysis indicated what the problem was and what he had to do about it, and he realized that he had lost his concentration because of unresolved feelings about beating the number-one player.

This is what we mean by identifying the tensions interfering with play. Gottfried was able to restore his mind-body equilibrium by focusing on performance without worrying about strokes, movement, moods, or whether he was winning or losing. His comments reflect the confidence all big winners have or acquire. Bjorn Borg expressed the same attitude himself early in his career after breaking a long losing streak against Jimmy Connors. "The difference this time?" he said. "This time I was knowing I can beat him."[3]

Knowing you can win is different from being obsessed about winning. Preoccupation with being superior can lead an excellent player to such self-doubt that his game falls apart. This happened to Tom Okker when he played Bjorn Borg a few years ago. Borg and Okker had previously split four matches, but Borg was on the rise, and Okker had played little competitive tennis. Borg, just turned twenty, was continuously developing, but Okker, a seasoned veteran, had already reached his peak and was trying to maintain it. Borg won 6-2, 6-2, 6-2. An off night for Okker? Maybe. But why such an overwhelming difference in performance between two talented players?

When interviewed about the match, Borg observed, "Well, you know, sometimes when one player plays very well, the other plays very badly." In this succinct comment, he was acknowledging the impact of superiority/inferiority tensions on mind-body integration. The fact that Borg had been steadily racking up victories may have stirred up hidden doubts in Okker about his ability to win. If he was unaware of these doubts and channeled them into an overriding desire to prove himself superior, then the four split matches would only have increased his hidden tension, since they proved him *equal* but not *superior*. Unresolved tension can build up until mind-body integration collapses under the strain.

The emotions leading to a choke can be complex and hard

to accept. Some people have mixed feelings about winning—unconscious desires to lose—that get in the way of their conscious wish to trounce an opponent. Recently an outstanding Chicago player described a choking experience which revealed to him his hidden feelings of discomfort about winning. Playing in a singles match, he was leading 6-1, 5-2, anticipating an easy victory as he began to serve out the match. He won the first point, but when the opponent returned his next serve, his usually strong forehand failed with a sudden cramping of his hand. As he bounced the ball with his left hand before beginning his next serve, his right hand relaxed sufficiently for him to serve comfortably. In the ensuing rally, his hand cramped again, and suddenly he was down 15-30 with visions of losing the match. Only his forehand was affected. He bounced the ball a few seconds to give himself time to relax his right hand, and then served again. His opponent helped matters by netting the return of serve. At 30-30, realizing that his forehand was no longer functional, he purposely served wide to the deuce court and successfully cross-courted the return of serve with his backhand for a winning placement. At 40-30 and match point, his opponent responded to the pressure and overhit his return of serve.

After the match was over, his hand was as normal as ever, and no cramping occurred during the doubles match he played later that evening. When he reconstructed the sequence of events that led to his choking, it was obvious to him that the spasm represented a choke. He was able to link the chain of events in his mind: He had been playing smoothly *until he first consciously thought of winning;* as he began to serve out the match, he thought, "I've won—this guy's dead." On his very next forehand, his hand went into a spasm. (Our guess is that his forehand was affected because it was his strongest stroke.) This dramatic body failure was directly connected to his ambivalence about winning. Consciously, he had been enjoying the idea of victory, but his deeper, suppressed self was afraid of winning, and influenced the muscular tension in his hand. He had felt overwhelmed by the cramping, and his practical, on-the-court solution kept him going, but it did not resolve the problem behind his choking. What did bring him closer to a solution was his introspection later about the experience. Once he realized that the fear of winning was a major factor in his choking, he could watch for the tensions it evoked during games, and eventually he was able to accept and work through these tensions to become a consistently better player.

The fear of winning is more common than might be expected. Consciously, we're all in the game to win. But the mind is complex. Achieving success may be experienced by some of us as a psychological loss, since success often means standing on your own without a feeling of parental love and support. Success may also symbolize superiority to the parents, and consequently the mind either imagines or senses parental hostility to making it on your own. This kind of unconscious interference can crop up at unexpected moments and destroy mind-body integration in a player who is—on the surface—determined to win.

Some of the deep feelings that can lead to choking are connected with a more direct feeling of disappointment in performance. You're just not performing well. You're not worried about winning or losing; you're looking objectively at your play, and you just don't like what you see. You're not playing the way you think you should be able to play. Tennis, along with many other sporting activities, is often a proving ground for effectiveness. Each tennis player has his own idea of how he should be moving and stroking the ball. But excessive concern with trying to perform up to a perfectionistic standard can end up destroying mind-body integration.

You can suspect that this is your problem if you often get intensely angry with yourself on the court. The extreme perfectionist gets frustrated and enraged with himself when he is unable to achieve his goal of perfect play. Blowing up expresses his rage with himself, frustration with his inner self rather than with external conditions. The explosion of rage can represent a reaction to the fragmented mind-body feelings that are present when things aren't "together" inside the player's mind. He may direct his rage toward a close line call, but that's not where it originated. Explosive rage may simply represent a form of temper tantrum, with the player reenacting the outrage of the child who discovers that the world is not exactly the way he wants it to be. Such a player is reexperiencing old childhood frustrations. He says, "There's nothing wrong with trying to play perfectly," but he will always be running a futile chase, trying to use his tennis racquet to repair his inner frustration at a world that never lived up to his expectations.

Mind-body integration breaks down when the player is unaware of these tensions and suppresses them, then tries all the harder to play perfectly. He gets distracted easily, can't function automatically, becomes self-conscious, and usually ends up restless and apathetic—he's bored. It's not enough for him to win; it's not enough even to play well; if he hasn't played up to his ideal, the game is over for him.

As with all the other hidden tensions, the thing to do is be aware. Notice your feelings; after the game think about them. How often do you get irritated with yourself on the court? How often do you condemn yourself for having played poorly? Be aware that this irritation has deeper sources, that it's an outbreak of a deeper rage and disappointment that is an essential part of your psychological makeup. As you become more aware and connect the superficial feelings with your deeper suppressed tensions, you will find yourself more able to manage your inner tensions and less prone to channel them into an irritation with yourself that brings on choking.

Raul Ramirez was able to do this. Once he became aware that his perfectionism was ruining his mind-body integration, he worked out an effective technique to deal with his irritation after a bad shot. He was somehow able to dominate his momentary rage by remembering the last point he had played well, and savoring the feeling of mastery it had given him. This took the dynamite out of his rage and kept his mind and body together.

Much of the perfectionism found in tennis players represents a search for mastery directly related to a wish to master internal tensions. The relentless effort to perfect a backhand volley is really the perfectionist's attempt to feel better inside, to master the internal tensions that can interfere with coordinated functioning. But the only way to master those tensions is to take them on directly by becoming aware of them. Of course you should practice that backhand volley—but direct your *real* concern toward the tensions that drive you toward excessive perfectionism.

The perfectionist strives for ease of functioning above all. When things go really well, the strokes flow, the player feels free to devote his attention to carrying out his game plan, and tennis becomes a thinking person's game with a striking absence of self-conscious concerns. Practice and drills are essential to achieve mastery, but something else is essential too: awareness and identification of the deeper tensions that make you the person you are, that define your tennis style with its strengths and deficiencies.

So far we have stressed the importance of identifying the tensions that interfere with mind-body integration and lead to choking. We have mentioned some examples of on-the-spot assertive action that can help you manage your feelings on the court, and we have suggested some of the typical conflicts that create the subtle tensions that cause choking. When you suppress your emotional tensions, your body and intellect lack the emotional input necessary for them to work together toward sound planning and effective stroke execution. But when you acknowledge your aggressive or narcissistic conflicts, and understand the emotions they evoke, then you can begin to deal with your tensions effectively.

How Can You Solve Your Choking Problems?

Seeing things from a psychological perspective is the first step toward developing an effective repertoire of behavior to deal with your feelings on the tennis court. Being psychologically tuned in to yourself will keep you alert to the tensions interfering with your mind-body integration, and will help you to work out effective styles of assertive action for managing those tensions. You can learn a great deal about managing your emotions by observing the problems of other players and the solutions they find. This will suggest new possibilities for identifying and solving your own choking problems. We emphasize the word *suggest* because none of the examples we've cited is *you*. Each player has different psychological reasons for choking, and each player must work out a personal style for managing aggressive, sexual, and narcissistic tensions behind the choking. You can get ideas by watching how the pros do it. You'll see Ilie Nastase, whenever he is called for footfaulting, almost disdainfully ignore the linesman and quickly toe the line to serve again. Nastase wants to reestablish his serving rhythm as soon as possible. If he gets it going and starts to win points, you won't hear a peep from him. But if he starts to play poorly, then he may openly express his irritation at the linesman or appeal to the audience for support.

Watch Rod Laver, when called for a similar infraction, as he takes time to find out in detail the way in which the linesman says he footfaulted, and only then continues play. Laver, unlike Nastase, needs to take time to calm his emotions while he tries to resolve the problem by understanding what went wrong. This allows him to take corrective measures without worrying about being penalized again for a similar infraction. Laver's method can also interrupt his opponent's rhythm (although this is not his intention).

These are two different approaches for keeping your composure on the court; if they don't work for you, try something else that relates more closely to your emotional state when you are called for an infraction.

The guiding principle for solving your choking problem can be framed in a question: Are your techniques effective in managing your feelings so that you can maintain well-coordinated functioning? Knowing that aggressive and competitive conflicts affect mobility, balance, and weight transfer helps only when you are aware of your feelings and reactions. The step from suppression to awareness is a big one because once you are conscious of your feelings you can contemplate different solutions and try them out under different circumstances. The ideal you should aim for is a repertoire of behavior that allows you to make spontaneous corrections, improve your play, and change your game plan when things begin to go wrong. Results don't come easy or fast, but if you understand the process behind your emotional reactions, then you can recognize what's going on in your psyche and take steps to correct your problem.

It takes time to get a handle on your internal experiences. But once you get a feel for the pattern of your choking, you can plan your play to combat it. Organize a plan of play that recognizes the potential tension-provoking situations that may occur, and then watch how these situations affect you and how you usually respond. The problems that cause choking can be overcome only by understanding the interrelationships between mind and body; then, when you sense a choke beginning, you can get out of it, and play to prevent chokes in general. Just as a player develops checkpoints to see if something is wrong with his forehand or backhand stroke, so too can you develop emotional checkpoints that indicate when mind-body integration is faltering.

The tennis player's mental task is complicated: on the one hand, he must remain loose enough to respond intuitively to the court situation; on the other hand, a strategic correction may make the difference between victory and defeat. No stroke is automatic; just as all strokes require periodic review and correction, so do our emotional tensions need to be worked on constantly.

An analysis of your individual behavior, and what formed it, can be very helpful. What is your particular style, and what are the reasons behind it? Are you a slow starter? Do you rise to the occasion in the dying moments of the match, or is that the moment when you choke? Why? Specific psychological conflicts are involved, and your individual mind-body integration will reflect these conflicts in the way you manage your feelings on the court. Your early emotional and learning experiences have influenced your character structure and modes of tension regulation. Later learning experiences with a coach, friend, or teaching pro can either correct or reinforce your problems in dealing with tensions. You must look at yourself in depth.

Choking is, in one sense, the opposite of mastery. Bill Tilden once commented, "The champion never makes a simple mistake," but we could say that no one ever makes a simple mistake, in view of the complex psychological factors behind performance. A positive attitude undoubtedly facilitates genuine confidence in stroke production. Tennis players who are confident in their performance seem to have an innate feel for rhythm, mobility, and the momentum of play. They don't need to think about stroke production or mobility; they respond automatically, with an "instinct" for the game. All tennis greats have it, but this doesn't mean that they don't have to work at it. Tilden, who had the typical mobility problems of the big man on the court, became a keen student of the way his opponents moved, and through intense concentration and practice he gradually developed a solid confidence in his own mobility.

Some players rightly distrust excessive intellectualizing about tennis, yet over and over again we see instances proving the importance of rational thinking in tennis as an adjunct to understanding and working with emotional tensions. Tilden reportedly prepared four different game plans for difficult matches. A more recent instance: Arthur Ashe combined brains and talent to defeat Jimmy Connors at Wimbledon in 1975. Ashe studied Connors's play closely during the early rounds and realized when Jimmy defeated Roscoe Tanner that the only way he could beat Connors would be to hit a wide arcing serve, with a lot of spin but less pace, away from Connors's two-fisted backhand. Ashe came up with a wide slice serve, then followed it up by crowding the net as closely as he could, and hit winners against Connors's typically well-paced returns. His game plan worked, and Ashe became 1975 Wimbledon champion. The background to his strategic victory was his confidence in himself; he dictated the course of play, took command, and, except for a brief lapse in the third set, was never in danger of losing control of the match. He combined his confidence with rational thinking and came out a winner.

The rational mind has various techniques at its disposal to deal with sensations and feelings generated on the tennis court. A common method is to try to keep the mind clear by blocking out external distractions. The theory is that if you pay no attention to the score or line calls, there is less chance of being distracted by your opponent's playing style or his fussing over close calls. But this method won't work unless there is a true inward calm beneath your outward serenity. Active tension management is the only way to avoid chokes. Acknowledge all the feelings and thoughts (pleasant or not) that are going through your mind, and then sustain the tension they create long enough to enable your mind to work out more satisfactory ways of managing the tensions.

What does sustaining an experienced tension mean? To understand this concept, a sharp distinction must be made between *experiencing* and *expressing* feeling. The more directly and intensely a feeling is experienced, the better opportunity you will have to work out a solution. For example, it's better to acknowledge that you are angry or excited because of what has happened on the court than to feel vaguely tense. Experienced feelings are those emotional attitudes that emerge from our inner selves—our spontaneous thoughts and feelings. Some of them may appropriately be expressed; others, because of their ambivalent, sexual, hostile, exhibitionistic, or aggressive nature, are usually suppressed. The mind, in effect, judges against expressing the thought or feeling that is experienced. Whether or not we express a feeling depends on how acceptable we think it is to those around us, but also on how acceptable it is to ourselves. Again, the "acceptability" of a feeling depends largely on the type of experiences we have had throughout childhood.

With accumulated experience, you can learn the most efficient ways of dealing with your tensions. By acknowledging and working with upsetting or unacceptable feelings, you can sustain the tensions they create. There are no shortcuts. Being aware of and introspecting about your feelings is the basis for establishing a mind-body equilibrium that eliminates choking.

It's helpful to have categories of experience to review. The most important factors influencing players are court conditions, the quality of the opponent's play, the stakes of the match, your general psychological and physical state, the audience, and the person you're playing with or against. Let's take a look at these to find out what the mind's task is in dealing with the feelings evoked on the court.

Court conditions

Emotional sensations vary according to the playing surface, the court condition, wind, temperature, and lighting. Frustration can arise from serving into the sun, losing sight of a ball because of direct lighting, failing to return serve on a fast court, enduring arduous rallies on slow surfaces where patience is crucial, mistiming a ground stroke because of a wind gust, and countless other distractions that seem designed to interfere with rhythm.

Quality of the opponent's play

If your opponent is clearly superior, the first important question is: Does this make you play better or worse? It could bring on self-doubts and overidealization of the opponent— feelings that usually result in choking. Or your opponent's superiority could improve your playing if it makes you hit out, choose the best percentage shot, and take a "what-have-I-got-to-lose" attitude. An inferior opponent can give you trouble too; by unconsciously identifying with him and being easy on him, you may find yourself descending to his level of play.

The stakes of the match

Trying out for a high-school or college team, playing for prize money, or trying to build your ego by demonstrating your adequacy or superiority—these might be what's at stake for you in a match. The mind has different ways of signaling the tensions involved. The predominant emotions experienced by tennis players are anxiety, excitement, boredom, and rage. If you can't cope, your mind may be flooded with anxiety. If your primary motivation is to excel, dominate, and achieve mastery, then playing well can be exciting or stimulating. Boredom may set in whenever you sense a failure in effective functioning—instead of experiencing the satisfaction of a well-executed stroke, you feel apathy or restlessness. Sometimes beneath the boredom, or accompanying it, are feelings of shame or rage. You may blame these feelings on other distractions—business or personal problems—but usually the true cause is the internal failure in mind-body integration that allows these external problems to interfere with your play. The stake for many in tennis is achieving the pleasure of effective functioning. As one player put it, "When you crack the ball right, that aggressive discharge sets you on top of the world!"

General psychological and physical state

The player who comes off the court feeling excessively depressed may have started out in a state of excessive psychological need, expecting to symbolically solve his problems on the court. Tennis is a good vehicle for working out inner tensions, but too many unresolved tensions can set up a too-high expectancy so that if the game is lost, the player feels shattered. What can be done about this? There is no set solution, but it always helps if you understand what is going on. Sympathetic, insightful awareness of your reasons for investing too much emotion in a match will go a long way toward channeling tensions into more effective play.

Top physical condition is obviously a basic factor in good tennis playing. But remember that it can be offset by psychological tensions. Only when physical and psychological functioning are integrated can your body go to work for you.

Playing before an audience

Being evaluated or watched on the court can create special emotional problems unless you have a good understanding of how the audience affects your play. When others are watching, playing becomes performing, which can bring out your exhibitionism or your fear of being criticized. A hostile audience can get you down if you need encouragement and support to play well. Some players try to ignore the audience's reaction, failing to realize how boos or applause can influence mind-body integration. An audience brings out our primitive needs to be praised and cared about; when the audience is more interested in watching your opponent or another match, you may lose your concentration because part of you is worried about losing the audience's approval. Your relationship with the people who are watching you can have a decisive influence on your rhythm and may determine the result of a close match.

For these reasons, it's worth thinking about how audiences influence your emotions. It makes a big difference *who* is in the audience, since a special friend or family member will affect you differently than an audience you don't know. The wish to play beyond your ability is a common reaction when the stakes of a match are important and there is someone in the audience you want to impress.

Nora, a promising seventeen-year-old junior, was being scouted in a high-school match for a college tennis scholarship. She wanted to impress the college scout with her serve, but as the match progressed, she kept double-faulting and lost the first set because of two service breaks. Without realizing why, Nora was putting so much pace on her serve that she lost her rhythm and kept serving long. Although she checked her ball toss, thought about the wind conditions, and started throwing the ball closer to her body, she was unable to correct her serving problem.

When all her checkpoints had failed, she concluded that something else was wrong. She reluctantly decided to abandon her flat first serve and use more spin, realizing that by the time she won the battle within herself, she might lose the match. She narrowly won in three arduous sets.

When Nora reviewed with her coach the failure of her serve, she explained how she had "tried everything" she could think of to regain her rhythm. She knew she had increased the pace of serve, but wasn't sure why. Her coach shrugged it off, saying that she had just tried too hard. But Nora sensed that there was something more to her problem—more than just her wish to impress the scout in the audience.

The scout had evoked an exhibitionistic conflict that went back to the time when Nora was a self-conscious nine-year-old learning to play tennis from her father, and trying to impress him. She now vividly recalled how her father had laughed at her awkwardness when she had tried to coordinate the ball toss and service motion. Playing the tournament match, with the scout somewhere in the crowd, had brought back her memory of her father yelling, "Without a big serve, you'll never be a tennis player." Nora had been determined to prove to the scout (a symbol for her critical father) that she was a good player, but she also resented feeling prejudged, and this led to her mind-body failure. She had lost her rhythm because she was unable to modulate her exhibitionism.

By reviewing your court experiences, as Nora did, you can learn about the emotional tensions influencing you when you feel that you're on display and being judged. Nora's checkpoints had been incomplete; the pressure of the audience had evoked exhibitionistic tensions leading to a choke that she couldn't correct during the match. But by working over her feelings about being judged, and the anxiety evoked by her need to impress the scout, Nora found a way to influence her frame of mind whenever she was subsequently watched, and in this way she achieved greater mastern of her serve.

Family tennis

Playing with a family member creates another set of emotional problems that can cause choking or prolonged periods of poor play. Unconscious emotional attitudes are bound to surface. A typical pattern that arises is a lapse in concentration, followed by rage because you're playing poorly, and then a helpless, dejected attitude. Nothing seems to help.

Playing against a parent is always difficult. Many players never realize that beating a parent at tennis may be too loaded for their psyche to handle. Adolescents in their early teens usually play poorly against their parents because of their unconscious desire to maintain their childhood view of parents as idealized figures.

> Jason, a fourteen-year-old intermediate-skill player, always enjoyed the prospect of playing with his father. But whenever they played, Jason became exasperated because his game fell apart. No matter how hard he tried to concentrate, something kept him from playing his best. His father eventually guessed the problem and took Jason aside to discuss it fully with him. Together they talked of Jason's feelings about winning or losing against his father, and how these feelings seemed to be affecting his game.
>
> For a while, Jason continued to play poorly against his father, but soon he found himself bending his knees more, getting ready for his strokes sooner, and staying with the stroke from the point of contact to the end of the follow-through. Without consciously realizing the changes occurring in his body movement and posture, he began to prepare and execute his strokes for better results. His game improved dramatically, resulting in enjoyable rallies, close games, and pleasant experiences for father and son.

Sometimes tennis and family life don't mix. You may get bored playing with your sibling, child, or spouse because it's simply not a match. Say so, and don't play with that person; otherwise you'll spend many frustrating hours on the court, and tennis will become a drag. Family life carries with it important responsibilities and commitments; don't make tennis one of them. If you and your family enjoy playing tennis together, either competitively or as teacher and student, then go ahead; if not, watch out!

If you play doubles with a family member, it's helpful to think through the potential tensions that can interfere with your play. Problems come up when tennis players bring their family tensions onto the court. When there are sexual problems with a lover or spouse, a missed overhead or a bored expression may set off a chain of emotional reactions that don't belong on the court. By being aware of the tensions that may arise in family play, you may be able to anticipate problems before they ruin your game.

One simple way to identify your tensions in family tennis is to compare your tennis experiences with different partners. If you usually avoid playing doubles because you're afraid of letting your partner down, but have no problem playing doubles with a family member, the family relationship may provide a source of support that you need in doubles play. But if the tennis court becomes a battleground for working out emotional differences in your family life, then you should stop playing tennis with your family.

In dealing with court conditions, your opponent, your stakes in the match, your psychological and physical capabilities, the audience, or your family, approach your experiences with insight, feeling, and an open imagination. Much more is going on inside you than on the court. Let yourself feel what's going on; watch your patterns of tension regulation and try to attune them to your needs on the court. If you have conflicts with your exhibitionism (like Nora) or are frightened about the destructive potential of your aggression (like Jason) or are prone to any of the emotional tensions that lead to choking, what steps should you take to combat your problem?

1. *Being aware of your feelings* is sometimes difficult, but it's necessary. If you're not aware during the match, try to get in touch with your feelings afterward. The important thing is whether you can recognize the possibility of disturbing emotional tensions as the cause of your choking problem.

2. *Expanding your awareness* is the key for real progress in combating the choke. It may sound easy, but the natural tendency is to look for an excuse for your poor play, rather than digging deeper or exploring recurring patterns of choking. The mind protects itself from deeper emotions because they are distressing and sometimes socially unacceptable. Nora expanded her awareness by recalling the first important audience in her budding tennis career—her critical father. In the next chapter, on mind-body integration, we'll talk more about the

mind's resistance to acknowledging the painful emotional experiences from the past that can ruin your play.

3. *Working with the cause*—the disturbing emotional tensions that lead to conflict—is the essential step for achieving mind-body integration and self-mastery. If you practice and drill with an audience watching you to gain experience with your exhibitionistic tensions, then you will be able to try out your own methods to master these tensions. Whether you choke because of superiority-inferiority conflicts or because of anxieties over winning and losing, you can use each game you play as an experiment in self-mastery. By adding to your body skills a list of emotional checkpoints, you'll find you're on the way to combating the choke.

The Slump,
Or the Prolonged Choke

Players today are aware that their personal psychology influences their tennis performance, so that they have good days and bad days. But if the good days become fewer and farther between, the player is headed toward a slump. In one way, the slump can be considered a prolonged choke, as it is simply an extension of the bad playing caused by poor tension regulation.

We're all familiar with slumps, not only in tennis but in every area of work or play. Business executives, housewives, and schoolkids have slumps. We know that they usually go away sooner or later. But a lot of matches can be lost while you're waiting for a slump to "go away."

What can you do to pull yourself out of a slump? As with the choke, the answer is to become aware of your feelings and find out how they affect your play. The slump may be harder to deal with because it can create a vicious cycle of slump leading to depression leading to more slump leading to more depression, and so on. It's important to come to grips with your reaction to a slump, and the first step in attacking the problem is to acknowledge it—to recognize, unequivocally, that you are not playing well. Then try to think through the psychological meaning behind your slump. In doing this you must separate the primary cause of the slump from the secondary cause.

The *primary cause* is the one we're looking for—the suppressed tension that threw you into the slump.

The *secondary cause* is the depression and frustration that you feel in reaction to the slump. These feelings help to prolong the slump, but they'll subside if you can get at the primary cause.

The primary cause of a slump is usually hard to find, even though sometimes it's an obvious problem that makes you wonder why you didn't see it before it ruined your game. If you're worried about business or schoolwork, you may be allowing that stress to destroy your game. If your kids make you feel guilty because your tennis takes you away from home once a week, your tensions about them may be causing you to "punish" yourself by falling into a slump. If you have any kind of personal problems that you can't set aside when you walk onto the court, stop and look at the way you handle them as a likely cause for your slump.

Most articles on slumps explain them away by saying that the player is overtennised or bored and needs a rest. But the slump is rarely due to something as simple as fatigue or boredom. Both can be factors, but they must be understood psychologically. If a player is in a slump because he has "lost interest" in tennis, we must ask: Why does getting the ball over one more time than the opponent seem tedious where before it seemed a challenge?

> A fine junior player, who thought he'd try the summer tours to see about his chances to make it as a pro, found that as the spring came closer, his enthusiasm faded. He went into a slump that he couldn't shake, and he couldn't even get up enough interest to fight his slump. So he decided to wait another year to go on the summer tours. During the summer he played only occasionally; then in September he got back his old "feel" and enthusiasm. He forgot about his slump and played

well throughout the winter, with the goal of taking the tour for sure the next summer. But in the spring he again fell into a slump and began to wonder if he would make the summer tour after all.

He was too close to the problem to notice the obvious: For some reason he didn't want to play the tour. When his parents pointed out to him that he seemed to be avoiding the tour, he realized that they were right. Consciously he was eager to compete; but unconsciously, a repressed fear was holding him back. He was afraid that he wouldn't make it. The fear of finding himself inadequate had been so threatening that he couldn't risk doing badly, and so he had lost his enthusiasm and fallen into a slump to avoid the test of his powers.

The fear of failure is a common cause for the slump. It's a fear that we don't want to face, and so we escape from it by going into a slump. We don't *want* to slump, but we have little to say about it; our unconscious mind has taken the reins. An unconscious conflict interferes with effective tension regulation and expresses itself symptomatically, perhaps in poor timing. Mind-body integration is shot.

This player gave up the idea of the summer tours and settled back into his usual excellent playing. Without the fear of top competition, his spring slump disappeared. He was satisfied with the knowledge that he was not cut out for tournament pressure. Some players react differently when they find fear of failure lurking behind their slumps. If a player is able to look for the deeper meanings behind his fear, he may come to a self-understanding that will overcome the fear. *Why* is he afraid of failure? What feelings and childhood memories does he associate with his fear of failure? How do these feelings affect his tennis game? Dealing with the meanings behind such feelings can improve your game. Maybe our junior player will come back and tackle his fears in a few years.

Sometimes a slump is not a true slump in the sense that it is caused by simple body problems. A player who is bored by inadequate competition will gradually slump into lazy habits if he is the type of person who needs to be challenged to keep his strokes at their best. Or a player who gradually gets out of shape may go into a slump because he simply isn't able to get to the ball in time to prepare his strokes; one thing leads to another, and before he knows it he's lost his timing. If the player can be objective and honest with himself, he will be able to diagnose the problem as a physical one from the beginning, and then look for the psychological tensions that led to the physical problem.

In both the choke and the slump, personal conflicts cause tensions that lead to failures in mind-body integration. Identifying the conflicts and working with them will help you to deal with these failures. If you are aware of the deeper tensions interfering with your performance, you can train your mind and body to work harmoniously at the Total Tennis level.

·2·

Mind-Body Integration

Total Tennis requires the harmonious functioning of mind and body. Their dynamic interplay directly determines the quality of your performance; when they are working together optimally, your game is bound to improve.

Effective bodily functioning is the most obvious aspect of mind-body integration because it's where we most clearly see results. Bodily functioning is sharpened by the use of drills, constant practice, body conditioning, and lessons. Proper hand-eye coordination and good coordination between footwork and stroke production are indicators of high-level bodily functioning. Without a certain level of physical performance, one can hardly expect to become more than a mediocre player.

The functioning of the mind is less obvious in tennis, since we can't see its workings; sometimes the player himself is unaware of how his mind has influenced his play. Intellect plays its role through court strategy, game plans, corrections, analysis, and judgment. But as everyone knows, our emotions influence our intellect, as the mind functions not only through intellect but also through emotion. Emotion affects spontaneity, attitude, involvement, and the direction and concentration of psychic energy. Body and mind are the two factors in effective functioning, but since the mind has two aspects—intellect and emotion—there are actually three factors involved in mind-body integration. All three—body, intellect, and emotion—are equally important determinants of the quality of play. Each one influences and affects the whole: sound footwork and a well-placed ground stroke are not effective without solid strategy; a game plan won't work if you're emotionally conflicted; feeling confident and emotionally together won't improve your play if you haven't practiced enough.

In order to integrate bodily functioning, intellectual knowledge, and emotional attitudes, each of them has to be examined and set into effective motion. Let's look at them separately to see how each works with the other two for mind-body integration.

Bodily Functioning: Improving Your Play Through Practice, Drills, and Conditioning

Your body influences your play. Are you tall? Do you move well on your feet? Are your hands strong? Do you have difficulty moving backward to retrieve a lob? Think about how your body's strengths and weaknesses affect your play. Unlike other sports like basketball or football where physical size is very important, tennis requires no ideal physique. But your physical features are important in determining how you play and how you should approach practice sessions, drills, and conditioning programs. Part of improving your play is determining exactly what your body can do and can't do. Look at the features of your body and think about how they influence the way you play. But don't stereotype your body— remember that short players like Rod Laver and Chuck McKinley played the big game in the same style as Pancho Gonzalez and Jack Kramer.

Since your body determines much of your play, you must respect its limitations and develop its potential. Practice, drills, and conditioning programs can help improve your reflexes and strengthen muscle groups so that you can achieve your potential, but it's important to consider how effective these methods are for your needs. Hitting with a friend may improve your strokes, or you may need to drill to overcome a particular weakness. You may need to strengthen your muscles. Since your aim is to train your body to function in a specified way, you should first assess whether your body has that capability and whether the practice sessions, drills, and conditioning program you plan to undertake will be effective in achieving your goal.

Practice and drills

Practice is essential for good form and timing. Through practice you accumulate experience that helps you know your strengths and weaknesses. Though practice sessions lack the drama of match play, they offer the excitement of intense concentration and a chance for mastery.

Does practice improve your game? How? What's the difference between playing for four hours a week, and practicing two and playing two? When you practice, your aim is self-improvement. Your focus is different; instead of trying to figure out how to win the next point, you can pay attention to making your strokes more effective. Or you may just hit a variety of strokes two or three times a week. In practicing ground strokes you may detect a weakness in your forehand crosscourt and decide to hit only that stroke. Bill Tilden coined the phrase "intensive practice" to describe the work of mastering one stroke to the exclusion of all other considerations. (He devoted four grueling months solely to transforming his backhand into an effective aggressive drive.) Some players improve more rapidly if they practice a variety of shots and focus on a weakness only when it becomes obvious; in this way they take advantage of the mind's unconscious integrative capacities and the benefits of more varied play.

Unfortunately, many players find that continued practice is boring. If their play reaches a plateau at which they stop improving, they don't look forward to practicing as much as the successful player does. Part of the hard work of practicing is riding through such difficult periods in the hope of achieving a breakthrough, but the answer to overcoming the difficulty often requires analyzing the feeling of boredom when you practice, rather than doggedly continuing your practice sessions. When you can't overcome a weakness, it's sometimes better to stop trying for a few days and then come back to it with a new perspective, after your mind has had the time it needs to understand what's gone wrong.

Practice is a step toward identifying problems and working out solutions. Besides the essential role practice plays in developing skills, it can also help you become aware of your limitations and what you can do to compensate for them. Sometimes continued practice leads to the discovery of a recurring problem; you may then need a drill to improve your play, or a lesson with a teaching pro to help you correct the difficulty.

Strangely enough, the benefits of practice are not obvious to everyone. Vic Braden, one of this country's most experienced tennis teachers, feels that many players simply are unable to improve their game no matter how much they practice. He cautions younger teachers to avoid promising their students too much. John Newcombe is similarly pessimistic; he advises many players with weak backhands to accept their limitations. It's possible that both Braden and Newcombe are influenced by their own experience. Despite the help of Pancho Gonzalez and others, Braden has never felt confident about his forehand, and Newcombe has never been able to use his backhand as an offensive weapon. He has ingeniously compensated, however, by developing the famed "Newcombe Shuffle," which combines his great anticipation with his strong forehand to enable him to return second serves by running around his backhand and taking the serve with his forehand.

Learning a new maneuver to compensate for a shortcoming is one solution, but it's not the only one. It's important to keep your mind open and realize that a physical weakness can be either improved or overcome. But nothing can be done until you acknowledge you have a problem—and acknowledging and identifying the problem is more difficult than it sounds. Most players will recognize that they had a certain problem on a certain day, but they may avoid coming to grips with an ongoing weakness in their play. It's only human; it's very hard to step back and take stock of your shortcomings without using excuses. This is why many leading tournament professionals attribute their improvement to helpful, objective comments they receive from friends. You have to be able to look at yourself very objectively or listen to someone who can assess your weaknesses.

Harry Hopman, the most successful Davis Cup coach in the history of tennis, developed a set of drills for his Australian Davis Cup players that helped his team members feel confident about making any shot they might come up against in match play. Hopman's training dictum is "Match practice for match play." He considers it a waste of time to just hit from the baseline, because the strokes never come up the way you practiced them. Hopman also teaches a repertoire of shots to cover predictable match-play situations.

Hopman uses a mind-body perspective in his teaching by carefully evaluating the relation between the court abilities and temperamental character of his players and by helping his players identify their problems. One of Hopman's greatest achievements as a coach was his work with Neale Fraser, another former Wimbledon champion and the current coach of Australia's Davis Cup team. Fraser's left-handed twist serve was his strong point. His natural feel for spin, combined with Hopman's tutelage, made it easy for Fraser to go through the three-step process of practice, mastery, and perfection. Hopman's strategy was to improve the improvable and compensate for what couldn't be improved.

The aim of practice is improvement of your overall game. But to work on the fine points of your game, it's necessary to extend practice and focus it in a drill. Drills are a concentrated form of practice designed to help consolidate mind-body integration. Good drills provide repeated experiences with stroke and footwork problems, familiarizing the mind with the tensions that accompany performance. And good drills give you a chance to develop your mental and physical reflexes.

Like practice, drills can be boring if they're not done correctly or if they have no meaning for the player. One possibility is tailoring your drills to your interests by choosing particular shots and situations that come up repeatedly in *your* tennis matches. Don't choose a drill just because you read about it in this month's tennis magazine; choose it because you feel the need for it. If you're working toward a concrete goal, you'll get excited about the drill because it will give you a sense of coming closer to a double reward: mastery and victory.

The greatest value of drills is that they give you a self-confident feeling that you can rely on your body. Drills lead to quickened reflexes and automatic responses. When your responses are automatic, your mind is free to link the experience of the stroke with the strategy of the game plan. This is how drills can lead to creativity.

Physical conditioning

Practice and drills, however, are not enough if you're not in top physical shape. Physical demands for competitive play are far different from those for recreational play, but either way you want to be able to stay with your opponent, and you want to avoid stretching a hamstring every time you run down a lob. The American Orthopedic Society for Sports Medicine estimates that 50 percent of sports injuries are due to the player's inadequate preparation. They have found that you're less likely to get injured if you're young and if you play advanced tennis. This is partly because young and advanced players are in top physical shape. But if you're an amateur player who can't turn the clock back, there is still something you *can* do: improve your physical condition by following a conditioning program.

Most tennis players are motivated by the game and its goals rather than by the desire to develop their bodies. It's the *play* of the game that attracts them, along with the chance to master a skill and compete. In tennis, the value of being in topflight condition is not so obvious as it is in football, and tennis players often avoid calisthenics and conditioning programs; their tennis suffers for it.

The player who is in good physical shape is able to get to the ball sooner than the player who must put self-conscious effort into his physical movement. A top college player told me that when he ran the cross-country during high school, his tennis game improved dramatically. After six months of long-distance training, he became aware of a significant improvement in his concentration on the tennis court. "I was just always *there*," he said. "It was like I didn't have to move to get to the stroke. And I never got tired on the court. As I played, I sensed that I was stronger than my opponents."

Being stronger than your opponent also makes you *feel* stronger than your opponent. This feeling plays back into your game. It's especially important in outdoor matches, where endurance is a big determinant of the outcome. It's always easier to play a long match in an air-conditioned indoor court than outside under a hot sun. But many players become so intent on practicing a specific weakness that they forget about the importance of preparing themselves physically for the problems of outdoor play.

> A top player who had been out of serious competition for a few years decided to make a comeback. He worked hard on his strokes, particularly his spin second serve. He arranged to play in a few local tournaments and then took off for a series of tournaments. He had to play two and three rounds of qualifying matches a day and found that he was as good as the top college players, but in crucial moments he felt weak and choked. After losing a number of three-set matches he naturally became discouraged.
>
> Two factors led to his feeling of discouragement. His improved second serve gave him no particular advantage, since his competitors all had good second serves and no outstanding weaknesses. Consequently, each match became a bitterly contested battle in which he felt he needed "something extra" to dominate and win. The second factor was his physical condition. Since he was used to indoor play, the summer weather became an irritant and he found himself plagued with physical fatigue owing to the hot, humid conditions. Since he had neglected to train *physically,* he was weak on an outdoor court. He ruefully concluded that he had not anticipated the changes from indoor to outdoor play. But he had also neglected the complete mind-body perspective—*the way you feel physically will influence your mental attitude.* His morale was destroyed as he found himself to be no competition for the superiorly conditioned (and disciplined) college players.

Whether you are an aspiring high-school or college player, or a weekend tennis enthusiast who enjoys recreational play, your physical condition will determine the quality and enjoyment of your experiences on the tennis court. Make no mistake about it: tennis, like any other competitive sport, is a physically demanding and strenuous activity. You can do a great deal to maintain top physical condition and prevent tennis-related injuries. Warm-up exercises to stretch your muscles and joints are essential to facilitate mind-body coordination and to reduce the danger of muscle or ligament tears and sprained joints. Don't expect too much of your body too soon. Some tennis teachers and coaches recommend cardiovascular exercises (jogging, jumping rope, running in place) to accelerate the warm-up process.

Once you are on the court, make sure you feel warm before you take off your warm-up outfit, especially in air-conditioned indoor facilities. In outdoor play, when the temperature drops during the late afternoon or in the evening, put your warm-up jacket back on.

Along with prematch and on-the-court exercises, a regular program of off-the-court calisthenics will help improve your play and reduce the possibility of injuries. High school and college tennis coaches complain that only a few of the younger tennis players are in top physical condition; these coaches have to get their team members into condition as well as work on strokes, footwork, general court strategy, and game plans for different opponents. The better tennis players excel because of their superior coordination, quickness, endurance, and greater physical strength. Weight exercises to strengthen your forearm, wrists, and leg and back muscles will help you hit stronger serves and deeper ground strokes and volleys. Well-developed forearm and wrist muscles are essential for racquet control. Rod Laver credits his strong backhand volley to constantly squeezing a tennis or squash ball to increase his hand's muscle strength and build power into his grip.

Some tennis players view coordination and quickness as a natural talent that can't be acquired. But as Bill Tilden demonstrated, a rational approach along with intensive practice *can* improve footwork and mobility. By understanding the ball's spin, you can better judge your timing and footwork.

To improve your mobility, skip rope, do short wind sprints, vary your speed as you run in place, and practice taking large steps followed by short ones.

The mind-body approach is especially relevant for coordination problems. If you are aware of your body movements, you can work toward coordinating an awkward ball toss with your service motion or modifying the rhythm of your forehand backswing for proper weight transfer.

Players who cover the court well are those who know where to run and how to get there fast. Like Evonne Goolagong, they may be blessed with natural speed and graceful movement. But if you aren't as fortunately endowed as Evonne, you can still learn to move well on the court by paying attention to your body sensations as you practice and drill, moving right, left, forward, and backward. Jimmy Connors covers the court extremely well despite his lack of natural speed and agility. Don't let his huffs and puffs fool you as he scurries across the court to chase down a forehand—he's already anticipating when he will change his stride to quick, short steps so that he can move his weight into the ball. He has learned to move effectively, and so can you.

Many players do not appreciate the interdependence of practice, drills, calisthenics, and physical-conditioning programs. It's hard to accept the principle that *your body determines your play.* But if you recognize what your body can and cannot do, then you can set to work to improve your quickness and strength, and thereby enhance your pleasure and success on the tennis court.

Mind Functioning: Improving Your Play by Using Your Intellect

Many players say that tennis is a mind game. Using your mind to psych out your opponent by changing the pace is one good game plan that aims at interfering with your opponent's rhythm. Another mind aspect of tennis is keeping relaxed on the court to avoid choking. A third is self-discipline; in playing "percentage tennis" you look for the right shot to approach the net, or you control your natural instinct to wallop the ball when you realize your opponent is using your pace to score winners with his returns.

Intellect and *emotion* are the two aspects of the mind that determine mastery and success in playing tennis. Once you know the strategy and tactics of the game and are aware of the emotions that can interfere with your concentration, you can achieve mind-body integration. Just as mind and body must work together for tennis mastery, intellect and emotion influence each other in getting your body to perform the way you want it to. Even if you have practiced a stroke, you will make unforced errors if your intellect and emotion are not working harmoniously. Rational thinking plays an important role in your strokes and footwork because so much of tennis requires anticipating your opponent's next move while you're coordinating your own muscular movements. Emotion is equally important in allowing your body to work effectively.

The effectiveness of any stroke depends on mind-body harmony. Practicing and then "letting your body do it" works for a natural stroke like the backhand volley, but you can improve it by making a conscious effort to extend the racquet head and intercept the approaching ball. As you prepare and execute the stroke, pay attention to your emotional reaction. If you are gun-shy at the net, then your rational planning should include practice drills to overcome your fear. If you train yourself to keep your eye on the ball as you extend your racquet, you won't flinch—despite your inner tensions—when a doubles opponent drills the ball down your alley. Two-on-one volley drills, beginning at the service line and then moving closer to the net, will improve your agility and reflex time. To achieve the self-confident feeling that is essential for mastering all your strokes, the best frame of mind is a self-assertive one in which you naturally follow your own initiative.

Solutions for your mind-body problems on the court can often come by recognizing the role of your emotions, and by thoroughly understanding tennis strategy and tactics. Intellect and emotion can hardly be separated. You can learn the overhead smash in a step-by-step routine, but if you have an emotional problem with your aggression and are afraid of "the kill," then you'll never feel comfortable smashing the ball, or you'll develop a hitch that interferes with your overhead stroke.

We will next discuss the role of intellect in tennis; later, we'll consider the gamut of emotional factors that can influence your play. Keep in mind how intellect and the various emotions relate; in many instances, our examples, although emphasizing one aspect of the mind, will of necessity include the other.

Intellect refers to the thinking you do before, during, and after a match. Before the game you plan your strategy. During a game you try to figure out how to earn a point, how to counter your opponent's strategy; if you aren't performing well, you consider changing your game plan. After the game you analyze how successful your strategy was. You also use intellect when you read books on tennis and incorporate their ideas into your approach to learning and mastering tennis.

What's the best way to learn court strategy and successful tactics? The learning that leads to mastery comes from your *experiences* on the court. When you realize what you can do and what gives you trouble, and how you respond when your opponent hits a deep serve or a sharply angled volley, then you have a basis for conceptualizing court strategies. Your experience is your essential source of information. To develop your feel for the game, try to integrate your experience with your understanding of the mechanics of stroke production. If you can't bring your experience and understanding together, you will eventually get bored with the intellectual side of tennis.

Thinking on the court

Even the most intelligent players usually do very little original or creative thinking when they're on the court. At best, they play with a prearranged game plan and use one or two checkpoints to keep their strokes fluid and consistent. Most of their thought is taken up with concentrating on watching the ball and trying to win the point. In tournament competition, during a break on the odd game the player may spend his time toweling off or just trying to stay loose.

If you reflect about your on-the-court thinking, you'll soon discover that you don't intellectually perceive a great deal of what's going on, partly because of the tension of the match. Halfway through a set you may finally realize that your opponent is killing you with his overhead smashes; either he is playing well, or you are lobbing badly. But the simple thought process necessary for you to realize what's happening may easily be blocked in competitive play.

Sometimes your game plan or your emotional set about an opponent interferes with your on-the-court thinking.

> Two friends were playing a match in which the superior player was losing. When the score reached 2-5 in the first set, the superior player finally realized that he was being passed at the net whenever he came up on an approach shot to his opponent's backhand. He changed his strategy and eventually won the set 8-6.
>
> In the post-mortem analysis, the players discussed the course of the match. The superior player said that for some unaccountable reason he had not been able to figure out why he was losing: "Suddenly, like a flash, I realized that you were hitting better off your backhand than you usually do. I just hadn't been expecting that."

What the superior player meant was that he had been following a strategy based on his *anticipations,* not on *reality.* The superior player's pre-game set, based on previous experiences with his opponent, had resulted in his stubborn refusal to acknowledge what was happening on the court. Tilden advised players to go into every match with more than one game plan, to take care of such contingencies. The idea is to stick with a winning game plan, but to switch to a more appropriate strategy when you are losing.

Most of your thinking on the court is automatic. You may

be aware of getting the racquet back to prepare the stroke and concentrating your attention on hitting through the ball. However, it often takes some time before you become aware of your pattern of play. It is much easier to watch others play and figure out what's going on in their match than it is to observe your own play. A big step to improving your thinking on the court is to develop self-observing techniques that you can rely on when you are playing. Don't be obsessive about it. Watching your strokes too closely produces inhibition and thus interferes with mind-body integration. You must trust your body. However, in your practice sessions, if you observe your emotional reactions and integrate them with what you learn about the mechanics and aerodynamics of tennis, then you can develop checkpoints, based on your kinesthetic experiences, to get your strokes back into the groove. Set your intellect to work on these steps:

1. While learning or improving strokes in pre-match practice sessions, think about your emotional reactions, sensations, and kinesthetic experiences so that you can develop checkpoints to make your strokes smooth and consistent during the pre-game warm-up session and the match.

2. Avoid an overly perfectionistic approach to errors: if you make a mistake, try to do better the next time but don't worry too much about it. However, you are making repeated unforced errors with the same stroke, then go over your checkpoints and try to figure out what's gone wrong.

3. Use checkpoints you can feel. If you can't concentrate on rotating your shoulders for a passing shot, feel the tension of your bodily movement and use that tension as a reminder to rotate your shoulders.

It's helpful to use both physical and emotional checkpoints to adjust your play when something goes wrong. The less experienced player may need to check his service grip, foot position, toss, and follow-through, while a tournament player concentrates only on his rhythm as he serves; both players are linking physical checkpoints to body experience to improve the serve. If you feel tense or emotionally blocked when you try to hit a hard, flat serve, then you need emotional checkpoints to monitor your frame of mind when you play. After a well-executed backhand chip return of serve, do you feel pleased or do you harbor hidden resentment because you had visions of hitting a magnificent topspin return? Your emotional attitude is as important for good strokes as bending your knees and checking your grip.

4. If you still have a problem, change your game plan. *Assume you are not perceiving something,* and wait for a flash or some other subjective clue that will help you to make the integration you are lacking.

5. If you don't solve your problem during the match, sleep on it. Then go back and do another post-mortem analysis, this time thinking about deeper sources of interference with your mind-body integration.

Strategy and planning

Game plans are based on court strategy. Strategy requires thinking through your best choice of shots in relation to your opponent, the court surface, and the physical conditions (indoors—low ceilings; outdoors—sun, wind, and humidity). For every stratagem you need a repertoire of strokes to back you up; there's no point in rushing the net against a player's weakness if you don't trust your net game. Your game plans and court strategy should begin with a careful assessment of your strokes.

Players trained on hard surfaces or grass learn to hit their ground strokes flat; clay-court players usually learn to slice their drives or use exaggerated topspin for added control, since pace is less important on a slower surface.

When you review your strokes you should evaluate how well each stroke will stand up under the pressure of match conditions. Roy Emerson, the former Australian Davis Cup star, used to hit his forehand so flat that his margin of error was extremely small. There was little room for improvement in the stroke, and he was prone to error if he tried for too much with it. When Harry Hopman convinced Emerson to develop some topspin on his forehand drive to improve the margin of error, Emerson's consistency improved significantly. Hopman points out that before Emerson modified his basic stroke, he was falsely accused of choking; once Emerson improved his basic forehand drive by adding topspin, he was never accused of choking again.[1] The problem was in the basic construction of Emerson's flat forehand: It demanded the timing and balance that he was capable of, but on a tough angle or against a deep drive his flat forehand was inconsistent.

After you evaluate your own strengths and weaknesses, you should carefully devise your game plans using the following criteria: (a) the plan is within your capabilities, (b) the plan is well suited to the playing surface and the physical conditions, and (c) the plan takes into account your opponent's strengths and weaknesses.

An extreme example will illustrate the importance of these points.

> A local junior player with a good, consistent topspin forehand was scheduled to play (for the second consecutive time) a superior, nationally ranked all-court player, who had good ground strokes, an excellent serve, and a good net game. The first time they met in clay-court competition, the match was a rout. The superior player pounded against the local player's almost nonexistent backhand, especially on crucial points, and when it was all over the local junior felt he had been lucky to win three games in two sets.
>
> An older club player, who had watched the first match, suggested a simple strategy that turned the tables around in the second match. The plan was to play everything to the superior opponent's forehand to avoid his backhand cross-court returns. In the first match the local junior had tried to take advantage of short balls by hitting his forehand deep to his opponent's backhand (not realizing, perhaps, that his own weakness was his opponent's best shot). The veteran club player noticed, however, that the nationally ranked player's timing was so good that he could take these balls on the rise because of the clay

surface and return them cross-court deep into his opponent's backhand side of the court. The club player recommended that in the second match the local player use more topspin, but with *less* pace. Now the local player met his opponent on equal terms, and his natural competitive instincts kept him in the match on the crucial points he had previously lost. The final score, a 6-2, 6-3 victory for the local player, did not tell how close this match really was, but it did prove that a well-thought-through change in game plan can reverse a result.

Tennis is often compared to chess inasmuch as both games involve judgment and planning that take into account tactical considerations. The chess player repeatedly ponders: "If I move here, what's my opponent's best counter?" The local junior player in the instance above didn't realize that hitting his forehand drive as a reverse cross-court, or down the line with pace, played into his opponent's strength, allowing him to exploit the local player's weak backhand. The local junior had not been aware of the pattern that the club player had noticed in the first match. He had had a game plan, but the more points he lost, the harder he hit the ball. He did not have an alternative game plan, nor was he able to think through the pattern of play his friend had observed.

In a more evenly matched contest between two good juniors, one of the players was noted for strong ground strokes and excellent passing shots; the other had a more complete game, but with no outstanding strengths. His coach observed that the opponent's ground strokes had a clear-cut pattern: he tended to hit his first ground stroke with fair pace, and then hit each successive ground stroke with increasing pace (as if he were more confident each time he hit the ball). The coach concluded that this was the key factor for the opponent's development of his rhythm; accordingly, he devised a game plan for his student that was deceptively simple and obviously designed to interfere with the opponent's mind-body integration. The plan was to come in on *everything—right away—*on first serve, on second serve, and on every return of serve. The result was a surprisingly easy (though physically exhausting) 6-3, 6-3 victory for the coach's student. After the match was over the coach mentioned his observation to the losing player's coach, who had not detected this recurring pattern in ground strokes in competitive play.

Sometimes adverse weather conditions will force you to adjust your game plan in a way well suited for playing against your opponent.

A good weekend player told me that on a recent vacation he played the teaching pro of the resort hotel and was easily beaten in straight sets. A few days later they arranged to play again, and this time, in a close match, the result was reversed. After it was over, the player realized that he had won because he had been forced by the wind to come up with the right game plan. To control his serve he had increased the spin and reduced the pace. His opponent's strokes were now less effective because they had relied too heavily on the previous pace; consequently, the reduced service speed had neutralized the effectiveness of the pro's ground strokes.

What can we conclude so far about game plans? First, you may need help to observe your play. A teaching pro or coach can help, but sometimes a relatively unsophisticated tennis player can help you discern the pattern of your play. Second, both player and coach may fail to see a problem, especially in competitive play. Third, a well-thought-out game plan can help you turn a match around or dominate play. Game plans assume a basic understanding of the mechanics and purpose of each tennis stroke. This knowledge is essential for a full grasp of court strategy; without it, your observations on the court are robbed of meaning, and you cannot expect to play creatively.

The relationship of
stroke analysis to game plans

Here's an example of how proper understanding of a stroke can aid in strategy. Both the one- and two-handed backhands are used for many purposes: to keep the ball in play; to return serve, either by chipping the ball low so your opponent cannot make an offensive shot, or by hitting out to gain the initiative; to attack by hitting cross-court or down the sideline; as a passing shot (against an approach shot in which the opponent rushes the net), either by a flat drive or topspin, or by an offensive or defensive lob; as an approach shot (against a short ground stroke or weak second serve); as a means of maneuvering your opponent out of position by a flat drive to open the court; as a drop shot (angled or down the line) to pull the opponent out of position or to bring him to the net and force him to hit a weak return; and as a purely defensive drive to keep in the point when your opponent has the initiative.

The current popularity of the two-handed backhand provides an interesting opportunity to examine, by contrasting it with the one-handed backhand, the way knowledge of a stroke is incorporated into a game plan.

In doubles, the one-handed backhand return of serve from the deuce court is regarded as the most difficult stroke in tennis because the stroke goes against the grain. Few players can turn quickly enough to make a full drive, so the best percentage play is a short chip, low enough to force your opponent to volley up. The opponent at the net, however, may move to poach as soon as you turn your shoulder. Thus the chip is a shot that requires exquisite timing and control; otherwise your net opponent will quickly volley your return for a winner. Once this pattern became clearly established, a strategy for doubles evolved in the form of a dictum: *In doubles you must get your first serve in at least 90 percent of the time—and* always *to your opponent's backhand.* Consequently, players with strong flat first serves hit their first serve as a modified second serve. They took pace off the ball, added spin, and tried to place the ball deep to the opponent's backhand. Players who have exceptionally strong forehands and good chip backhands occasionally employ a counterstrategy: they run around their backhand, take the ball on the forehand, and if they can time their stroke properly, aim to return the ball with a cross-court drive. The counter to this counterstrategy is the wide-angled second serve to the opponent's forehand, in anticipation of the shift to the left (as the opponent prepares to run around his backhand).

With the coming of age of the two-handed backhand, this doubles strategy is changing because of the differences between the two-handed and one-handed backhand. This is particularly evident in the problems of the deuce court player returning serve. Because of the basic differences in the mechanics of the two strokes, the ad court* player with the two-handed backhand is in a better position to return serve with a flat drive, but it is extremely difficult to hit a reverse crosscourt to the deuce side of the court or control a chip return from the deuce court. The average player still faces a difficult task, but the two-handed backhand is rarely as weak (in players of comparable strength) as a "weak" one-handed backhand. Many tournament players with two-handed backhands return first serves with an attacking drive rather than a defensive chip. Sometimes, especially against players whose two-handed backhand is their strongest stroke, it makes sense to serve wide to the opponent's forehand.

Percentage tennis and court strategy

Tennis has its own logic. For each stroke there is an appropriate counter that can be understood by considering the mechanics of the stroke and the aerodynamics of the ball's flight. You may hear John Newcombe on TV comment, "That's an intelligent shot," as he describes the play of the top pros. Newcombe analyzes the choice of stroke in relation to the court conditions, the opponent's preceding stroke and court position, and, occasionally, the score.

The basic logic of tennis comes from an analysis of what your strokes can and can't do. This analysis must also be applied to your opponent's choice of strokes; if he returns your preceding drive defensively with a slice or chop, you can either take it on the rise (which requires near-perfect timing) or wait until the spin dies (at the top of the ball's arc). In the case of an overhead smash, if you try to return it with a forehand or backhand drive (especially when you're buoyed up

---

* The ad court is the left, or backhand, side of the court (assuming the player is right-handed).

by guessing which way the smash will go) you will usually be unable to time the stroke. Thus the majority of counter-attacking drives are either netted or hit out of court. A better percentage play against an overhead smash is to lob.

Experienced tennis players develop a repertoire of replies to different strokes. Against a volley the best answer is usually a ground-stroke passing shot, not a lob. Against a strong ground stroke hit with pace and momentum, the best reply is a modified slice drive to impart backspin and decrease your opponent's pace.

The logical elements of tennis must be linked to your psychological perspective and understanding. When Bjorn Borg defeated Ilie Nastase at Wimbledon a few years ago he decided to restrict his passing shots to drives (not lobs) when Nastase took the net, because he realized not only that this was his best percentage shot, but also that Nastase had one of the best overhead smashes in tennis. Throughout the match Borg stuck to his plan of ground-stroke passing shots, even when Nastase had the angles covered so well that Borg had no chance to win the point with a ground stroke. He persisted because he felt that there was little possibility of winning a point with a lob against Nastase. Borg opted for a game plan that was logically sound and helpful in keeping Nastase from establishing his rhythm.

Many court strategies are simply predetermined sequences of shots whose purpose is either to earn the point by aggressive tactics forcing a defensive reply, such as responding to a lob with an overhead smash, or to change the pace to interfere with your opponent's rhythm.

Practice and drill consolidate such sequences so that you can focus your attention on what your opponent is doing. Three or four cross-courts to your opponent's forehand and then an angled cross-court to his backhand side *challenges* his rhythm. Against a slower player, or during a point in which you have seized the initiative, alternate cross-courts, if hit with good depth and pace, will eventually hamper your opponent's attempts to cover the court. Opening the court in this way is a good stratagem because, with proper execution, it frequently forces a short reply that you can exploit with another cross-court and rushing the net.

Planning means designing your strokes with a sound court strategy in mind. The player who plans his strokes improves his timing. When you decide, "I'm going to return this ball cross-court with extra spin and as deeply as I can" then you get to the ball a split second earlier.

Ideally, you should know the answer to these questions each time you hit a ball:

> 1. Can you drive this return, or should it be stroked with medium pace? (Once you have decided, be absolutely resolute—don't push your return.)
>
> 2. Do you understand the logical basis of your decision?
>
> 3. What length of return do you need to maintain the initiative (or keep the ball in play)?
>
> 4. How does your choice of strategy affect your opponent's rhythm?

This last question challenges you to think through the full consequences of your actions on the court. The idea of using psychological understanding in tennis is sometimes restricted to "psyching out" maneuvers that can interfere with your opponent's rhythm. It needn't be. You can use psychological understanding to help you decide on a game plan or a change in tactics during the match. Changing your pace or your strategy may improve your own play as well as interfere with your opponent's winning pattern.

> During the second set of a long tournament match, the losing player noticed that his opponent was playing each point a little more quickly than before. Was he tired? Was he afraid, since it was now late afternoon, that the poorer light would interfere with his vision or sighting on overheads? Or was he anxious in some way about winning, and over-eager to close out the match? The losing player realized there was no way to guess what was behind it, but he immediately decided to slow the pace and take as much time between each point as he could. He had correctly assessed that something was interfering with his

opponent's mind-body integration; his change in tactics paid off as his opponent proceeded to make a series of unforced errors and lost the match in three sets.

It is a mistake to play each point rigidly according to your pre-game plan. Although Tilden was a proponent of following a well-thought-out game plan, he realized that each point had to be played with a mini-plan in mind, as the player asks himself, "Do I attack, defend, or maneuver on this shot?"

Part of the problem of planning strategy is anticipating your opponent's reactions, especially if he is losing. He will change his tactics if he sees that he is playing to your strengths rather than probing your weaknesses. A complete game plan should include contingency variations. For example, you might say to yourself, "If I rush the net, he may try to chip my second serve and come in to take the net away from me; therefore, I'd better make sure I'm getting most of my first serves in, even if I have to take something off the pace to increase my accuracy."

Tactics

Tennis tactics are best determined by a thorough consideration of: court conditions (playing surface, sun, wind, temperature, and humidity); the strengths and weaknesses of your opponent's strokes; the score of the match; your opponent's game plan; and the logical choices for each point. Your choice of tactics may emphasize one of these factors according to the needs of the moment.

In a well-lighted, high-roofed, indoor air-conditioned tennis court, a junior player warmed up with his opponent and soon found himself hitting out as hard as he could on each stroke. After winning the spin for serve, he paused for a moment to think about his pre-game plan in light of what he had observed about his opponent during the warm-up session. "The guy sure likes to hit," he thought. He also realized that his opponent's drives barely skimmed the net, suggesting a low margin for error. Although he wanted to hit long drives with pace to his opponent's baseline, as he had been doing in the warm-up, he concluded it might be wiser to use slice and spin and to vary the depth as much as possible.

On his first serve he decided to use his spin second serve into his opponent's backhand and try to slice the return of serve to bring his opponent to the net. His opponent drove the serve down the middle, offering no reasonable chance to slice the return; instead of driving the return back cross-court as he normally would have done, the junior player lobbed deep to his opponent's backhand, forcing a defensive reply to keep the ball in play. Instead of attacking, he sliced the ball with undercut, angling it to his opponent's forehand, deciding to alternate from forehand to backhand so that his opponent would not be able to groove his strokes.

As one spectator commented, it looked like a long, drawn-out clay-court match. Two and a half hours later the match ended in victory for the junior player, 7-5, 7-5. His tactics had paid off. He never gave his opponent anything he could really hit out on.

Tactics aimed at exploiting your opponent's weaknesses or interfering with his rhythm are successful only if you stick to the precepts of logical tennis. Varying the spin and depth makes sense as long as you don't give your opponent a short ball or try to slice his underspins. Your choice of tactics may vary from a relatively simple idea (as in the above example) to a more complex plan that takes into account your analysis of the player's form, his court temperament, and whether you are winning or losing.

Weaknesses in your opponent's stroke production can be diagnosed by analyzing his form and movement. Does he keep his racquet head high on his low volleys? Does he move better to his right or left, up or back? Does he turn well when he hits his overheads? If you find that your opponent is chipping your second serve and coming into the net behind it, you can try two good plans: either slow down your first serve to increase your accuracy and then try to take the net from your opponent, or hit your second serve as hard as your first to make it more difficult for him to chip and come in after his return.

The purpose of analyzing your opponent's form is to exploit his weaknesses and press him into unforced errors. An unforced error can discourage your opponent more than a winning placement on your part which he can rationalize as, "He made a good shot. He deserves that point—but I'll get the next one." Your opponent can only blame himself for netting the ball or hitting it out of court. Since roughly two-thirds of all points in top-flight tennis end in errors rather than in winning placements, it makes sense to think through your court tactics with this factor clearly in mind.

In both singles and doubles a sound tactical principle is to keep the ball in play rather than risk a winning shot that has a high chance of going out or into the net. Some players think of hitting hard as taking an unnecessary chance; that's incorrect, unless your strokes are unreliable whenever you increase the pace. Your attacking shots should have a high percentage of success. If they don't, you are making a mistake in your choice of strokes.

Tilden comments, "The best tennis tacticians play a defensive game with an offensive mental attitude."[2] His main recommendation is to play the percentages, and scrutinize the opponent's strokes to exploit weaknesses. But he also stresses the importance of going for the winner whenever the right opportunity presents itself. He suggests occasionally hitting out to extricate yourself from a defensive position on the chance that you might make the low percentage shot or startle your opponent.

Tilden also notes that the player who establishes the *tempo* of the match tends to dominate play. Watch Jimmy Connors as he prepares to serve or return serve. His four-bounce ritual before he serves, and his playing with his stringing so that he seems unaware that his opponent is ready to serve, help Connors to think about the next point at *his* tempo, rather than at his opponent's. Don't let your opponent determine the tempo of a match. On the other hand, a player's stalling on the court can interfere with the opponent's concentration and constitutes a breach of court etiquette. The good court tactician has a clear understanding of the difference between stalling and taking an appropriate amount of time between points, odd games, and the end of a set. Subtle psychological interplays often occur over the pace of the match, leaving one player feeling that he is dominating his opponent, and the other feeling he is being manipulated or controlled.

Just as important as scrutinizing your opponent's weaknesses is acknowledging his strong points—if only to avoid them. Borg did precisely this when he won the 1976 Wimbledon Men's Singles Championship final against Nastase in straight sets. To avoid Nastase's overhead smash, Borg repeatedly attempted ground stroke passing shots, rather than lobs. On points where Nastase dominated play, Borg, faced with a no-win situation, continued to attempt to pass Nastase at the net. This strategy averted Nastase's strong overhead and also prevented Nastase from developing a winning momentum.

If you are not sure about what your strengths and weaknesses are, and how they influence your play, then chances are you will be too preoccupied with your own game to detect what is working (and what isn't) against your opponent. Sometimes a spectator can turn a match around by simply pointing out to a player that he is being passed too often at the net and that he should change his game plan.

> One of the most agile, quick players I have ever seen was losing a match without knowing why. He dropped the first set 6-1 and began to complain that his knee was acting up. In this way he rationalized the failure in his strategy—rushing the net on every ball he could. His opponent's passing shots didn't seem that tough to this player, but somehow they were winning points! After the conclusion of the first set, the player's coach said two words, "Stay back," and the tide turned. The opponent's rhythm was disrupted by the change in strategy, especially mixing up the pace of ground strokes, and he soon made a series of unforced errors. The match ended in a 1-6, 6-1, 6-1 victory.

The change in game plan resulted from the coach's observation that the opponent seemed to be a good counterpuncher—perhaps he might not be able to take the initiative on his own. In the post-mortem, the coach commented that he would not always be around to come up with an answer for future problems, and he suggested that they try to figure out why the player didn't think of changing his strategy on his own. The player didn't have to reflect very long, although it had never crossed his mind during the match: "I didn't trust my ground strokes; I never do in a match. That's why I always rush the net when I'm losing."

The potential effectiveness of your game plan depends on your physical ability to carry it through and your mental ability to assess your opponent's strengths and weaknesses. Your body and intellect mutually influence each other: if you feel confident about your ground strokes *and* your net game, then you can *objectively* decide whether you will do better by staying back until you have the opportunity to take command of the net.

To sum up, court tactics require a thorough understanding of the mechanics of stroke production and the aerodynamics of the ball's flight in order to assess the effects of spin, depth, and pace. Scrutinize your opponent's form and footwork to assess his strengths and weaknesses. Play percentage tennis according to a pre-game plan that takes into account your own strengths and weaknesses as well as those you can detect in your opponent. Be prepared to stick to your plan; but don't be stubborn about changing it if you are losing. Be prepared to play each point logically, and be flexible enough to alter your plan when you sense you have figured out a better plan to beat your opponent. Don't be afraid to go for winners, but avoid the trap of going down to defeat with false courage by hitting out on everything. Use your head!

Understanding Your Emotions: The Key to Mind-Body Integration

The interdependence between bodily functioning and intellect is clear-cut: problems arise in competitive play that call for strategic planning and tactical maneuvers, both of which can be practiced and perfected by specially designed drills. But tennis mastery requires more than practice and intelligence. The best-conditioned, most strategically brilliant player sometimes cannot perform well because of emotions that influence body and intellect and interfere with the processes that lead to good mind-body integration. Your emotions can influence your assessment of what's happening on the tennis court as well. Intense, suppressed emotion will inevitably interfere with your rhythm. To achieve real mastery on the court, you should have some understanding of your needs for perfection and your conflicts about winning or losing, since repressed conflicts can prevent your making the observations necessary to integrate your body and intellect on the court.

Improving

Often the first step to self-observation is to get the objectivity and emotional support of a tennis coach or teacher. This step can be viewed as the beginning of a solution to a problem, even though the player may not be aware of his problem or of the steps that will lead to the ultimate solution.

Many players have a feeling that they have reached their best level of play, and that it would be difficult or unrealistic to expect further improvement. This feeling itself can lead to a standstill since your *attitude* is 50 percent of your game. The right psychological perspective will not solve all your problems, but eventually you should experience an unexpected breakthrough to a better game. The breakthrough can lead to a transformation.

Tennis coach Ray Price says that his student Chuck McKinley's breakthrough occurred when he mastered the jump overhead. Unlike Kramer, Gonzalez, and Trabert, who had the height and reach necessary to cover the net, McKinley is not tall; he learned to use his athletic ability to compensate for his lack of reach, and went on to become a Wimbledon champion. How does a player learn to work around his shortcomings and acquire a new skill? Is a breakthrough physical or psychological—or both?

Timothy Gallwey claims that the breakthrough can only happen when Self 2 dominates Self 1, when the player lets go of his self-conscious preoccupation about winning so that he can achieve the spontaneity and unified movement necessary for good court performance. Gallwey's viewpoint has considerable merit, but it understates the importance of identifying, differentiating, and overcoming specific physical and psychological problems that often interfere with stroke production and coordinated movement.

A breakthrough to higher levels of mind-body integration is often facilitated by a coach or teacher. Talent alone rarely leads to mastery. Even the great tennis star Ellsworth Vines attributes his meteoric rise to stardom to the help he received from his coach, Mercer Beasley.

> I hit very hard, flat shots and Beasley used to raise the net four to six inches in practice. He figured if my shots still went in, then during a match the net would seem very low *and I could really go for it* [author's italics]. Also he used to stretch canvas about a handspan wide over the top of the net and cut holes in it, and I'd have to aim through those holes to hit a shot down the line.[3]

Vines's talent and self-confidence were prerequisites to mastery; his coach provided that something extra to increase Vines's confidence so that his forehand became a reliable passing shot and aggressive drive.

Once you have acknowledged a particular physical difficulty, you must work with drills and conditioning programs—but you must also search for the things that interfere with mind-body integration. With the proper balance between physical and psychological factors, you will be able to develop your strong points and compensate for your weak points. As you practice you will find it necessary to:

1. Review your frame of mind before and during your practice sessions and matches.

2. Examine your reactions to specific shots and lost points.

3. Look for the psychological cause of your physical problem, unless it involves an absolute handicap such as height.

4. Think positively as you make the necessary corrections to deal with your shortcomings and the psychological motives behind them.

Because so much depends on the player's ability to deal with his own problems, not everyone can find a solution to every problem. Don't look for a single road to mastery. Mind-body integration occurs in silent and different ways. Some players learn best by taking lessons and thinking carefully about their learning processes; others work better on their own, with little introspection, but planning their practice sessions to achieve increasing mastery. Both these approaches can be combined in varying proportions in a program of lessons and practice. Unfortunately, players usually do not give enough thought to what ratio of practice and lessons is most beneficial for their learning and mastery. You may need more lessons, a different tennis pro, or more time on the court. But these factors in themselves do not cause a breakthrough. Breakthroughs occur only as the result of a new level of mind-body interaction. Establish the necessary conditions that will help you to learn, and then be prepared to allow sufficient time for your mind and body to put together new connections and become familiar with them. Don't be discouraged if you feel your game is stagnating. Often the first step to increasing mastery is acknowledging that you are blocked in your progress.

The way you learn to play tennis is not entirely in your conscious control. What you *can* do is use your intellect to understand how the mind and body work together and how psychological factors can affect your performance. Think about how you learn. Do you learn best on your own, or do you get into the same old ruts? Some players do well when they work with a friend; others respond well to authoritative guidance. What works best for you?

The best tennis players in the world admit that they have

their blind spots. Vitas Gerulaitis and John Alexander both commented that other touring pros told them they were serving weakly on their second serves. Of course, they could have seen this themselves, but the comments of others helped. Sometimes a friend's straightforward comment about something you're doing wrong can provide the stimulus for you to acknowledge the problem so that you can work on it. Before mind-body integration can occur—before you can hope to master that serve or volley that troubles you—*something must happen beneath the surface of your mind.* Think about this idea. No matter what your conscious intentions are, hidden emotional factors may block your attempts to develop smooth, well-coordinated strokes. You can't control your learning processes with rational thought, but by understanding your past and present learning experiences you can open your mind to higher-level learning.

Coping with frustration

When your emotions block your mind-body integration, you will feel frustrated, disappointed, and enraged; no matter how hard you try, you can't stop making unforced errors. Some good players never achieve their full potential because they cannot deal with their frustration realistically. They try to resolve inner tensions with quick solutions rather than take enough time to understand their problems and work systematically toward a solution. Although they may be aware that their play needs improving, they can't take the necessary steps. These players have a special problem in mind-body integration; they are not able to work toward a goal with sustained effort. Although they may be talented players, their wish for an easy solution precludes the concentrated effort that leads to mastery.

The best reaction to the frustration you experience in your efforts to achieve mastery is to take a realistic approach combining practice, lessons, studying strategy, and replaying in your mind your experiences on the court. You may discover that such a well-reasoned, disciplined approach goes a little

against your grain. Once in a while you may find yourself re-
senting the hard work necessary for mastery and success.
This attitude—which can cause lapses, slumps, or occasionally a total withdrawal from tennis—may be rooted in your
early childhood development.

Part of the mind feels it ought to be able to do *anything*—
with ease. It gives you a feeling of self-worth that tells you
that you can succeed in the tasks you set out to accomplish.
It's the force in your personality that can bolster your initiative when you are plagued by self-doubt. The person who pos-
sesses self-confidence has the best chance of achieving success. If he is also blessed with the ability to objectively assess
defects in his game, he can take the action necessary to solve
his problems on the court.

Consider the experience of frustration. Behind the feeling
of frustration lurks the haunting anxiety that you may not
achieve mastery; that you will remain frustrated despite
your best efforts. The mind cannot tolerate being helpless, or
anticipating feelings of helplessness, without signaling its
discomfort. On one hand, anxiety caused by feeling helpless
may mobilize you to work harder. Or it may bring out the
worst in you, including unrealistic grandiose schemes. It's
worthwhile to pause right now to describe to yourself how
you react to frustration. This is an essential step in mastering your inner tensions when you play tennis. Do you get
somber, while seething inside? Do you throw temper tantrums? Do you give up emotionally, or do you try harder? Or
do you look for quick, unrealistic solutions?

> An extremely talented tennis player took a job as a teaching
> professional in a leading tennis club in the northwestern Unit-
> ed States. But after six months of teaching tennis he became
> bored and dissatisfied with his game. To overcome these feel-
> ings, he decided to get into shape with the idea that the next
> year he would join one of the professional tours.
> After a week's practice he began to feel the difference in his
> timing and reflexes. But after some practice matches with the
> top local area players, he realized he would have to do much
> more work to be successful against tougher competition. He

worked intensely for another month, still with the goal of joining the tour the next year. As he thought about his decision, he had a flash of psychological insight that stopped him short. He realized that something about it was too impulsive. He became aware of his pattern of dealing with frustration. His frustration always led to depression and boredom, and to deal with these feelings he would come up with a grandiose solution—in this case, joining the tour. He now realized how unrealistic this plan was, especially since he had tried to accomplish it without giving himself adequate time to prepare properly.

He then started acting realistically to modify his old pattern of dealing with frustration. He reduced his teaching hours to leave time for intense practice, arranged to compete in local tournaments to sharpen his competitive play, and postponed joining the tour for another year.

Once you identify your own pattern of coping with frustration, the next step is to explore the emotion causing poor play. Tennis players who rage at themselves or berate their opponents are using tennis to relieve personal frustration. When they can't demonstrate their mastery, their self-esteem suffers and self-doubt clouds their perspective. Since their energies are focused on the frustration rather than on the underlying emotional cause, they can't detect the emotional conflict interfering with their play.

Some tennis players need the feeling of mastery for their psychological equilibrium. They are addicted to the game; if they don't play they feel restless and even agitated. Business or personal problems take second place to their interest in tennis, because when they are on the court and playing well, they feel protected from their deeper feelings of inadequacy. Hitting the ball right provides these players with the feeling that they can, by extension, master their other problems and frustrations.

Players with such deep concerns about their adequacy usually have a low frustration tolerance. They may flare up or literally have temper tantrums if they cannot achieve a feeling of satisfaction when they are on the court. As disconcerting as this may be for those who have to endure their behavior, the player having the tantrum suffers the most. Behind the rage reaction to the frustration of not playing well are deeper conflicts rooted in feeling worthless. These feelings of deep shame and personal humiliation are even more intolerable than poor play. Sometimes they lead to grandiose fantasies, setting up a recurring cycle in which the player goes from feeling absolutely resolved to quit tennis forever to feeling convinced he is on the verge of a breakthrough to mastery.

Players with deep-rooted problems about mastery are easily spotted and can become the prey of psychologically-minded opponents.

> In a mixed doubles match of a local tournament, one of the teams scouted their opposition and saw that the best strategy was to put as much pressure as possible on one of the opponents even though she had better strokes than her partner. They noticed that she was such a perfectionist that whenever she missed a difficult shot her concentration suddenly disappeared. She would make a series of errors, throw her racquet on the court, and hold audible conversations with herself in which she criticized her every move.
>
> The player with the short fuse couldn't tolerate the feeling of frustration she experienced when she missed a shot she felt she should have been able to make. When preoccupied in this way, it was impossible for her to regain her composure and use what she knew about playing percentage shots in doubles. The doubles players figured out enough about their opponent to put the pressure on her when she missed a shot, but then played the other partner if they sensed that the easily frustrated opponent had regained her equilibrium after making a difficult shot. Once they fully understood the pattern, they tried whenever possible to avoid challenging the short-fused player with a tough shot, because they realized this helped her to recover her equilibrium.

When you are feeling frustrated on the court because you are missing shots you feel you should be making, the sensible thing to do is to check your strokes to see if you have developed a hitch in your backswing or if you are having some

problem with your footwork. If you continue to make unforced errors, then look for a deeper answer to explain your
frustration. Identify your problem. Do you look for unrealistic solutions because you can't tolerate the feelings of helplessness or worthlessness that come from performing poorly?
The grandiose-fantasy solution leads to unforced errors, incorrect evaluations of your opponent's strengths and weaknesses, and inability to maintain concentration during the
match. You cannot achieve mastery if your mind-body integration is being clouded over by grandiose fantasies.

As always, solutions begin with acknowledging the problem. Even if you don't consider yourself a grandiose person,
consider the possibility that you are prone to the same grandiose fantasies you despise in overt egotists. If you find
yourself coming up with grandiose temporary solutions,
think carefully about how these fantasies get started in you
and how they interfere with your play. Stop and feel the frustration that pushes you toward magical solutions. Notice
how these "solutions" affect your mind-body integration. Do
you suddenly lose your cool when your opponent makes a
fine shot? Do you go for impossible winners when you are
leading in a match? Look for the pattern in your play. Compare your impatient play with your play when you've got it
together. As you analyze, you will get a practical feeling for
the ways in which your fantasies can interfere with mind-
body integration and divert you from problem-solving. Quick
answers occasionally work, but most of the time they barely
touch the problem. Frustration may push you to action, but
to achieve mastery you must deal with the problem underlying the frustration.

Competing

If your problems arise in competitive play, then your fantasies and conflicts about winning and losing may be the cause
of your frustration on the court. Do your emotional attitudes
about winning and losing interfere with your play? Among
the psychological pressures that can influence your game,

tensions about winning and losing create the worst havoc. If you are not performing your best when you compete, such a conflict may be disturbing your equilibrium. Confronting this problem is essential for achieving mind-body integration. If you fall into a pattern of errors, or find yourself in a slump, ask yourself whether winning—either in general or against a particular opponent—has some other meaning for you.

> In a men's doubles match, two juniors were playing against two older opponents. One of them, a nationally ranked senior player, was in his mid-sixties. The older team scored a close victory. After the match was over, the junior playing in the deuce court complained that he hadn't done anything right. He was especially disappointed in his forehand return of serve, which he had kept hooking far to the opponents' right, wide of their sideline. His partner agreed, but he thought the forehand return of serve had been even worse when the older opponent was at the net. The junior with the errant forehand sensed that "something" was wrong, but, at the time, he didn't ask himself whether he was experiencing a conflict about winning. A few years later he recalled this experience in a conversation with me: "You know, I was *afraid* of nailing that old geezer with my forehand. No wonder I kept hooking it." His fear of winning masked his apprehension that he would injure his opponent (who really could take care of himself).

The fear of the power of your own destructive aggression is an important internal pressure that can interfere with mind-body integration. Usually it takes a more disguised form such as a hitch in your service motion or lapses in concentration either on crucial points or when you are gaining the initiative in the match.

Motivation

There can be many motives for playing tennis. For those who play seriously and develop a love for it, tennis provides a channel for creative and aggressive energies. You may have taken up the game because something about its aesthetics interests you, or the sheer aggression in hitting a cross-court forehand or killing an overhead smash may excite you. Social and peer pressures to play, because of the current tennis boom, may have stimulated you to find out what it's like. But unless tennis provides you with an unconstrained way to express your creative and aggressive side, you'll soon lose interest. If you have personal conflicts that inhibit your self-expression on the tennis court, then you'll frustrate yourself by missing easy smashes or choking on your forehand.

In our culture, males are usually more comfortable than females about competing. A junior boy may boast that he "slaughtered" his opponent in straight sets, while a girl might say that she won because she played well and her opponent played badly. The psychological need to dominate is well cultivated in males, so they are more comfortable about expressing hostility and fighting for a point. A player told me that he had defeated a woman in straight sets, even though—as he conceded—her game was basically superior to his. Because he knew she had difficulty in expressing aggression, he had never felt worried about the outcome of the match. "I knew I would win after the first few games. She gave up on too many points. I knew I wanted it more than she did, and that's why I won."

Although many woman players are tenacious on the court and have a strong need to win, few women have the so-called killer instinct. Sometimes the difference in play between men and women is attributed solely to physical factors—people think that since men are physically stronger and faster, they play more aggressively. This fact leaves out the importance of conflicts about expressing aggression in tennis. In competitive sports—where winning is connected with dominance and feelings of superiority—men usually feel freer to express their aggressions than women do. Women who want to but can't play as aggressively as men, must examine their feelings about the parental and social conditioning that has led them to suppress their expressions of aggression. Each woman can understand more about her aggressive conflicts by reflecting on her personal, individual feelings about aggression.

Behind the struggle for victory in sports are primitive aggressive feelings that seek expression in sublimated form. Tilden compared tennis to boxing; psychoanalysts have analyzed tennis as a duel. Why? Because it is a one-on-one contest in which the goal is to break down the opponent's defenses, and to outmaneuver and destroy him. Winning can be equated with "*killing*" the opponent. A score of 6-0, 6-0 is equivalent to a knockout. And the defeated player often feels humiliated—he feels that the failure to win a game is proof that he's no good. Behind the embarrassment at losing may be a deeper psychological conflict. Some men have repressed any feelings of submission, which they equate (unconsciously) with homosexuality; they react to such feelings by trying to offset them with a macho attitude or a highly aggressive stance. Losing badly can touch off these feelings, and a player may feel humiliated since in his unconscious mind he feels he has surrendered to his hidden submissive desires.

Some male players, conscious of their struggle with their aggressive impulses, try all the more to get tough on the court and go for the kill. Other players, who fear their aggressive instincts, may choke whenever they feel threatened by the breakthrough of their hostile or sadistic impulses. There are also some players who obviously enjoy thrashing their opponents and can't contain their exuberance at the triumph of the slaughter. Rather than win a point in a straightforward manner, they prolong the rally and force their opponent from one side of the court to the other. They then may try to win the point with a dropshot to demonstrate the opponent's physical helplessness. Players with psychological conflicts about winning may also suffer from similar, yet repressed, sadistic tendencies. Losing is one way of keeping these upsetting impulses in control.

The abundance of theories to explain why one player wins and another loses has resulted in a great deal of pseudo-psychologizing about winners and losers. Many tennis players believe any match result can be explained by careful analysis of the strokes and strategies of the opponents. But when one player consistently wins the big points, or defeats one opponent after another despite having no overwhelming superiority in his form or strategy, he is viewed as "a good competitor," or people say, "He just has better nerves." The loser is dismissed with something like "He doesn't have the stuff of a champion." Probably every player has been accused of being a born loser at one time or another. Borg, Connors, Vilas, and Nastase have all been criticized about their inability to win the big ones. In any tournament of 32, 64, or 128 competitors, only *one* player comes out unscathed; the rest are fair game for the critics.

There are no born losers, but there are "made" losers—people whose competitive conflicts interfere with mind-body integration. Such players have choking problems or reveal a well-defined pattern of failure in close matches. Sometimes a good player loses to an inferior opponent because of a conflict about winning. This may also be your predicament; if you get tense in competition and lose to players you should be able to defeat, start examining your desire to win.

Some players thrive on competition, playing their best when the pressure is greatest. Rod Laver and Bobby Riggs are like this, and it's interesting to note that they both come from large competitive families. Riggs says he gets interested in a match only when it's close.

Learning to play competently is one thing, winning is another. Winners are always competent, but competent players aren't always winners, because something extra is needed for winning. It takes more than good strokes, top physical condition, and sound court strategy. You must also want to win, know why you want to win, and understand your competitive conflicts (if any) about winning.

Of course, almost every tennis player wants to win, perhaps more than he admits. Every stroke, every rally, every point, game, set and match has one objective: winning. Every second on the court you are competing, moving and hitting, trying to gain the initiative or win the point outright. The inner tension you experience becomes an emotional task to face with every stroke you play. Maintaining mind-body integration will keep the pressure on your opponent.

No player in the world can completely control his inner tensions; that's why the idea of flawless tennis is a myth. But by keeping aware of your feelings, you can maintain an equilibrium. You may sense a momentum building up when most of the points come your way. But when it's 40-15 and you're serving to close out the game, you can't help but think, "Just one more point . . ." That's okay. You want to win. But you must meet head-on your conflicts and anxieties about winning or you'll fall into a pattern of losing the crucial points.

Does competition scare you, stimulate you to play better, or make you fold up and withdraw emotionally? Do you *know* when you're choking? Look at your pattern of winning and losing points and matches. Does the natural buildup of pressure during a point lead you to unforced errors on your third or fourth ground stroke, or do you feel, as the rally develops, that you are mastering your strokes and enjoying the challenge of competition? If you begin to feel a physical fatigue that stops you from playing your best on each point, an emotional conflict about winning may be getting in your way.

Winning and losing patterns can fascinate, befuddle, and frustrate the players, coaches, and audience. Charting the sequence of points won and lost is a good approach to unraveling the conflicts and anxieties generated in the pursuit of victory. Here's how a player's account of the sequence of winning and losing points clarified the role of emotional factors in his match:

> This guy came *alive* whenever it got close! He won twelve deuce games, think of it! I played well enough to win—in fact, I think I came close to winning as many points as he did, but when the games were even, he played better on the big points. Whenever I was sure I had the game, he'd get out of trouble with a great passing shot, or he'd lob deep and cancel out my initiative. It's not that I was choking; it's just that he kept getting better.

The winner had that extra reserve that makes the crucial difference in a close game. For many such players tennis has a more personal meaning than getting exercise, demonstrating skill, or enjoying the game aesthetically. Though they probably enjoy these aspects of the game, they have an inner need to win that is not overwhelmed by their tensions about winning. Consistent winners are also more complete in their preparation for each stroke and more tenacious in sustaining pressure on the opponent. They usually bear down more on each rally and make a higher percentage of difficult strokes. Quite naturally the observer points to these factors and says, "That's why he won." But this is only a superficial observation; it leaves out the unconscious factors that influence the winning and losing of matches. Advising a player to concentrate harder treats only the symptom, not the disease. Every player knows the importance of keeping his eye on the ball. If someone reminds you to concentrate, it may help you momentarily; but your play will improve only when you figure out what is diverting your attention. The answer is tension, and often it's tension about winning.

Children and adolescents who have been encouraged or pushed on by their parents often have conflicts about winning because they feel they are achieving for their parents rather than for themselves. The motivations of players are usually more complicated than that, but the pattern is the same. The player feels he has the talent to play well, but he finds tennis boring. Winning has no personal meaning for him. Sometimes a sensitive coach can spot this problem and help a junior player work out his feelings about playing competitive tennis. If there is no objective third person to stand between the player and his family pressures, his game is unlikely to improve, and he may be accused of lacking "guts" when it comes to a tough match. Pressure is hard on the junior player who feels alienated from his parents. And then there are those situations in which the player's parent pushes and intimidates him into a fear of losing; he may win out of fear, but at a personal cost that leaves him feeling embittered and exploited. For these children and adolescents, tennis is a chore. Whatever satisfaction they achieve in hitting the ball right is canceled out by their inner feelings of alienation and of being exploited.

Being afraid to win may seem like a strange idea at first. After all, everything you do (consciously) is directed at winning. Maybe you're not aware of any conflicts about winning, but if you *want* to win and *can't* win, it's time to face the fact that some part of you does not want to win and is keeping you from winning. A friend of mine never (consciously) paid attention to the score, but always choked near the end of a match. He said he didn't care about winning. Actually, he cared enough to avoid it.

Look at how competition and jealousy were handled in your family when you were a child, and you may pick up clues to your present problems with competing and winning. One woman—an excellent player—would never have considered playing in a tournament a few years ago because she "couldn't tolerate the emotional pain of losing." When her friends asked her why losing a tennis game could be so important to her, she said, "It's not the game—it's losing. I can't stand to lose anything." She left it at this for years, but finally began to face the source of this feeling, as it had held her back at work as well as in tennis. "My mother," she said, "always did everything better than I could. She always made a point of how I couldn't do anything as well or as fast as she could. That's why I hate to cook; every time I bake a cake I'm competing with her, and invariably I lose again." Her mother's constantly putting her down throughout the years had left her with what she called "a gutful of suppressed rage" that she was afraid to let out for fear of losing her mother's love. Because of this, whenever she lost anything she was unconsciously reliving her mother's put-downs. Working on these feelings, she realized that she had more trouble playing tennis with women than with men, because women more closely symbolized her mother. As she faced up to these emotions, she started bringing them out onto the court and being aware of them *as she played*—working with them and analyzing them before, during, and after matches. She now plays the occasional tournament—and, incidentally, is much more comfortable and successful in her professional life.

Failing to concentrate on the court is one way of avoiding

coming to grips with your conflicts about winning. For some players the idea of winning evokes hostile feelings and thus stimulates them to guilt reactions. How do players deal with these guilt feelings? By carelessly throwing a match away (through nonconcentration) or by pressing too hard for shots they can't make. Don't expect an easy or quick solution for this problem. "Winning attitudes" and "better self-images" are only a partial answer. As Mark Cox, the British Davis Cup player, has said, "The secret of improving your game lies in learning to believe you can do it."

Sometimes a player seems destined to win his matches no matter what he does. He comes to net at the wrong time but still wins the point; he hits strong forehands, teeing off on the ball with his feet all wrong, but he still wins. It's as if he's trying to beat himself but can't. If you know a player like this, watch him a little more closely. You'll see that (1) he rarely fails to capitalize on his opportunities; (2) he believes in himself and knows that he'll probably win; (3) he doesn't feel guilty or shy about being aggressive; and (4) he enjoys the competition, even when points aren't coming his way.

Losing symbolizes helplessness and death; it evokes feelings of inadequacy, humiliation, and fear. Players who have deep conflicts about winning are often extremely embarrassed when they lose a game, because losing calls up their deepest concerns about being adequate. They may try to "justify" things by blaming match conditions. Try these excuses on and see if they fit you:

> "The sun was in my eyes."
> "My racquet was dead."
> "I've got a blister on my finger."
> "I'm having an off day."
> "The linesman was riding me."
> "I didn't practice enough."

It may be true, but it won't work as an excuse more than once or twice a year. If you find yourself rationalizing your losses more often than that, start thinking about what's behind your embarrassment at losing. And watch yourself if you get injured a lot. Frequent athletic injuries occur in players who fear failure or think they are over the hill, and the injury becomes the excuse for withdrawing from competition. Turning hostile feelings inward can cause you to become injury-prone—though most often it leads to plain old depression and lack of self-esteem.

Mastering your narcissistic tensions

Narcissistic problems commonly arise from overdependence on how others view your play, excessive concern about winning, or conflicts about your self-worth. They show up on the court in the form of temper tantrums, fears of being embarrassed, or an uncompromising need to play perfectly.

Many tennis players reveal their narcissistic conflicts in the way they interact with the audience. Because they need emotional support to maintain their self-esteem, they are especially sensitive to the way an audience reacts to their play. Such players often perform better when they are watched, but if the audience turns against them they become discouraged. When they lose a match, they blame it on the audience's hostility.

The support of fans and friends in the audience provides positive reinforcement, especially when the going gets tough. But if a player is worried about winning, he may become too dependent on the audience, and their reactions may divert his attention from his game.

Who's in the audience, and how do you feel about them? Many juniors play better if their family stays away, but others need their family's emotional support and like to prove themselves with mom and dad there to watch. As an adult, you may unconsciously react to the audience as if it were your family, and you may be trying to get reactions from the audience that you wanted to get from your parents twenty or thirty years ago. This idea may sound far-fetched or ridiculous to you, but it may be related to your problems. Try it out—compare your feelings about the audience to your feelings about your parents and see if you come up with any similarities. If you do, you have something to work with. And remember, whenever the audience constitutes a pressure for you, even though it's an external factor affecting your performance, the real problem may be an unresolved internal pressure about winning that is provoked and masked by the external one.

Players who are narcissistically stimulated by an audience sometimes grandstand to get attention. It can be hard to tell whether the player is going all out to win the point or merely playing up to the crowd. Even seasoned players sometimes win the sympathy of the audience and use this emotional support to carry them through to victory.

Audiences (especially in the United States) tend to side with the underdogs if they are appealing or attractive. Thus in apparently uneven matches, heavily favored players may find that they have two opponents—the other player and the audience. When the audience starts cheering for the loser, commentators usually say they are pushing for a closer, more exciting match. But they're also reacting to their own feelings about winning and losing. Many people prefer to identify with the losing player. And some players know how to use this.

> Fifteen years ago, in an international tournament, an almost unknown European was playing a top American player. The European, an affable, appealing person, played well but seemed outclassed; the American was running him ragged. But he took it well, complimenting his opponent's strokes as if he were an admiring observer. He seemed to be more interested in the aesthetic qualities of his opponent's game than in winning. The American won the first game with four straight serves, only two of which the European was able to put back into play.
>
> After changing sides the European, now firmly established as the underdog, faulted his first serve with a sluggish service motion. His opponent then returned his second serve so deeply that he could only lob it back, and the American put away the smash to go up love-30. Twelve minutes and seven deuces later, the European won the second game to hold serve. But the audience felt that the slaughter had only been delayed, since the American proceeded to win his serve again at love.
>
> With the score now 1-2, the players changed ends again, and something important happened: The audience began to clap for

the underdog, indicating their support and sympathy. Within minutes the quality of his play changed drastically—his service motion strengthened, he began to move with agility and speed, he covered the court well, and his ground strokes became so deep and consistent that the American could hit no more winners. After two exhausting sets the match was over, the underdog barely squeaking out the victory.

Throughout most of the match the underdog had the crowd's support. Was his style of play built around the audience's support? He had seemed on the verge of collapse, yet finally he was able to deal with everything his opponent could dish out. He never stopped admiring his opponent's fine play, and his win in the end seemed almost accidental.

This player's conflicts with his narcissistic, aggressive, and competitive feelings showed up in his passivity, his admiration of his opponent, and his underdog appeal to the audience. Reporters described him as appealing, dogged, and courageous, but perhaps he should have been credited as a superior strategist who was aware of his inner conflicts and tailored his style of play to them. His court presence and style of performance would predictably win from the audience the support that he needed to win the match.

This kind of underdog stance works more often than you might imagine. Sometimes in a closely contested match the losing player senses he needs something extra and calls a very close ball in his opponent's favor. By doing this, he wins the audience's sympathy and is able to turn the match around, using their support to buoy up his play. Is this contrived strategy? Yes and no. Few players who perform this way are fully aware of how their court style is related to audience interaction, but when it's pointed out to them they are not surprised. They like to describe themselves as counterpunchers, because they are not comfortable with the aggressive style of going out to win right from the start, all energies focused on the final result. Underdog players play that way because it comes naturally and it works best for them. They hide their aggressive side and narcissistically use the audience to help them bring it out.

Sometimes it's hard to tell whether you have played your

best; you can play well and still lose if your opponent is playing better. But because playing your best is often equated with winning, players become confused about the distinction between "winning" and "doing your best." Sometimes you'll end up wondering whether you lost because you played badly or because you were outclassed. Either way, it's more important to ask yourself how you react inside.

Players with narcissistic problems also tend to take their results too seriously. If they lose or play poorly they feel ashamed; if they're playing doubles it's worse because they feel they've let their partner down. These players often try to rationalize their errors because they can't tolerate the shame and embarrassment of having done a bad job. When players lose mind-body integration, they will often try to cover up their true reactions.

> One woman told me she had a problem in doubles play that never came up in singles. In singles she would shrug off her unforced errors and go on to the next point determined to do better. But in doubles, she always felt compelled to apologize to her partner each time she netted a ball or missed a put-away. During one match her partner sounded a little annoyed as he said, "Stop apologizing ... just do your best on the next one." That got her to thinking. Why *was* she constantly saying, "I'm sorry"? After all, she thought, she really wasn't sorry at all. She was feeling embarrassment and anger as she imagined that her partner was criticizing and condemning her.
>
> This player was projecting her critical attitude about her own play onto her partner; in effect, she was apologizing to herself for her failure to meet her own standard of play.

The player who is preoccupied with being a worthwhile person draws attention to his bad points through his self-conscious behavior. Such players suffer intensely; inside they rage at themselves for playing poorly. If you throw temper tantrums on the court, you'll easily recognize this problem in yourself; but often it's a more subtle, complicated pattern of self-humiliation.

> One successful tournament player showed an interesting pattern of winning and losing matches—a pattern that revealed

hidden narcissistic and aggressive tensions interfering with his play. Against tough competition he played well enough to just win, but every once in a while he lost to weaker players. He noticed this pattern and concluded that he was just having a letdown after a series of rough matches. Whenever this happened his "solution" was to drop tennis for a while and come back to it firmly resolved to practice and play harder against weaker opponents. This always worked for a few weeks, but then he'd fall back into the pattern of losing to weaker players.

When he talked about this with me, he became aware of two problems that he hadn't considered before. As a child he had always been "the star performer," while his younger brother was "sort of a jerk" who didn't do much of anything right. As he talked, it soon came out that in his unconscious mind he thought of inferior opponents as "jerks" and connected them to his brother. He realized that just as he had always felt sorry for his brother and tried to let him win at games occasionally, he was letting inferior tennis opponents win. As a kid he had felt an almost sadistic glee that it was his brother, not he, who was the "jerk." Feeling guilty about this feeling, he had repressed it, and it was now surfacing to interfere with his mind-body integration.

The second problem revealed more of the sadistic element in his pattern of close wins against tough players. Whenever he played stronger opponents, he fantasized about how easy they would be to beat. He would think, "Hell, I'll beat him in straight sets!" But again he ran into a guilt problem connected with his feelings toward his brother. For him, winning was the same as trouncing the opponent. Trouncing the opponent represented trouncing his brother, which he had always secretly enjoyed doing. His guilt about this caused him to keep the matches close to avoid embarrassing or humiliating his opponents. He could then shrug off his win and say, "I was just lucky, he might get me the next time." In this way he was reliving his childhood relationship with his brother and saying, "*I* didn't make him a jerk. I'm sorry that I'm so bright and he's so dumb; I'm not really happy about it."

Highly personal unconscious motives such as this are behind nearly everyone's tennis style. Making yourself aware of them is the only way to improve your style.

Sex and tennis

We read a lot about how sexual tensions can wreak havoc on your play, but little is said about the importance of getting in touch with the deeper sexual feelings that get played out on the court. Both heterosexual and homosexual tensions can create emotional conflicts that may ruin your game unless you have a good handle on the role of these emotions in your life.

You can tell if sexual tensions are interfering with your game by being aware of your fantasies and daydreams. When you play with someone of the opposite sex, do you lose your concentration because you imagine that the other player is sexually interested in you? Or do you feel vaguely anxious when you play with certain people? Your sexual fantasies and anxieties can help you to identify the deeper sexual meanings linked to your experiences on the tennis court. You may have unconscious conflicts about sexual adequacy that are expressed symbolically in the way you play. Losing can be equated unconsciously with homosexual submission; winning may be unconsciously experienced as a sadistic fantasy of torturing or beating the opponent. Sometimes mastery is unconsciously equated with sexual exhibitionism—the player then feels embarrassed about working hard on perfecting a stroke.

Sexual tensions often pose problems in tennis matches between men and women. Some women feel self-conscious about playing aggressively because this view of themselves conflicts with their feelings of being feminine. Many men feel inhibited about playing aggressively against women. They may feel humiliated if they lose to a woman, because they feel their masculinity is on the line.

If you realize that your game is being disturbed by your fears of winning, losing, or playing a certain way against a member of the opposite sex, stop and think about what is making you feel that way. Giving in to irrational sexual fears without ever becoming aware of them is a good way to destroy your game. Thinking through these fears and understanding their origins will help free your mind for better mind-body integration.

Here's an example of how being unaware of sexual tensions—in this case, homosexual ones—ruined a good tennis pair.

Joan and Brenda had won their women's doubles club championship for three consecutive years. Both women excelled at doubles and seemed to play their best tennis when playing with each other.

Joan first noticed a change in her feelings about playing with Brenda while admiring her partner's overhead smash. She thought, "I'll never be able to hit a consistent overhead like that." Over the next few months, her admiration increased in intensity and gradually changed to envy. She began to have mixed feelings about going to practice sessions with Brenda; she wanted to play with Brenda, but something inside her made her feel uncomfortable about it. In a way, she dreaded it. For a while she tried to ignore her discomfort with Brenda, but the tension mounted and became focused when Joan dreamt she was lying in bed with a nude woman. She awoke startled. Although she couldn't recognize the woman's face, she vaguely felt that the dream was related to Brenda. Upset, she tried to put the dream out of her mind.

Joan was unable to face the latent homosexual and envious feelings expressed in her dream of the nude woman. Instead of thinking it through and trying to make the connections between her hidden fantasies and her feelings about Brenda and tennis, Joan ran away from it. She canceled her practice sessions with Brenda and then decided to join her husband on one of his business trips rather than play in the next club championship. She knew that this would end her partnership with Brenda.

Joan's inability to think through her sexual anxiety resulted in the disruption of a pleasurable tennis relationship. Because she was unable to accept her envious attitude and the deeper sexual feelings it evoked, she could not deal with the problems that developed in her partnership with Brenda.

Whether or not we're aware of them, sublimated sexual tensions are always influential in the choice or rejection of a doubles partner. They are a normal and usually pleasurable component of human relationships and cause anxiety only when we're unable to face them and explore their meanings. If sexual tensions remain hidden from conscious awareness, they can exert a powerful influence on a partnership with neither person suspecting their presence. Many good doubles partnerships end with no awareness of the underlying sexual emotions that caused the problems in the relationship.

Guilt and depression on the court

One of the most self-defeating forms of emotional discomfort is unconscious guilt. It leads to depression and also destroys mind-body integration. Unconscious guilt is not the same as conscious guilt, although the two can coexist. Conscious guilt is the emotional reaction you have when you do something that you later regret. There's nothing mysterious about conscious guilt; you know you've done something wrong (like calling a good ball out) and you feel bad about it. If you then punish yourself by playing poorly, you're having an easily identified guilt reaction.

Unconscious guilt is a far more troublesome emotion. You don't have to do anything wrong to be plagued by it. It often goes undetected because it's a reaction not to reality but to your hidden fantasies. For instance, beating an opponent may touch off unconscious sadistic fantasies in you; without realizing it, you feel that beating your opponent is the equivalent of torturing or killing him. If this is happening in your unconscious mind, your guilt will cause you to play poorly as a punishment for your unconscious murderous fantasies.

The best way to detect the presence of unconscious guilt is to look for a recurring self-defeating pattern in your play. If hostile fantasies repeatedly interfere with your game, then unconscious guilt is probably the culprit.

> Brian, a player who had never achieved his full potential, invariably choked when pressed in a close match. His heart would skip beats and he'd lose his concentration. As his anxiety increased, he would imagine himself screaming at his oppo-

nent, "You son-of-a-bitch, why don't you give up this damn match?" He always hoped his opponent would make enough unforced errors to lose because he felt he couldn't finish him off by scoring winners.

Brian's palpitations and inability to concentrate properly (especially on the big points) were indications that an unconscious emotional conflict was interfering with his play. His recurring pattern of losing close matches resulted from unconscious guilt. Brian unconsciously wanted to kill his tennis opponents, and beating them on the court symbolized murder. But whenever he came close to victory, he also experienced tremendous unconscious feelings of guilt for his murderous wishes. By playing badly he avoided the effects of the unconscious guilt that would have punished him.

The situations that evoke unconscious guilt vary for each person. Players who are prone to guilt feelings usually suffer from a severely self-critical attitude, or they lack confidence in their ability to control their hostile fantasies. If you have days when you self-destruct on the tennis court, look for a guilt motif. Examine your spontaneous thoughts and fantasies, but don't let your aggressive fantasies frighten you, and don't be discouraged if you can't find the source of your guilt reactions. Understanding the deeper psychological motives that lead to guilt reactions may require extended self-examination or help from another person.

Depression is a common emotional reaction that usually results from guilt, low self-esteem (often due to personal failure), and frustrating emotional relationships. If you are severely depressed, you feel worthless and guilt-ridden; but moderate depression in the form of dejection, apathy, or discouragement can also have a destructive effect on your game.

Tennis players, like all other human beings, are prone to depression. If you're upset about something at work, or if personal problems have piled up to make you apathetic, your tennis game will be adversely affected. Most tennis players who suffer from depression realize that if their game goes sour, it's because they're too self-absorbed to concentrate on their play. But what happens when the tennis player thinks that his poor play is the cause, rather than the result, of his depression? Sometimes a vicious cycle develops: The depressed player may look forward to a couple of sets of tennis to raise his spirits; he only feels worse after playing because his timing, emotional awareness, and physical functioning are impaired by the depression he brings to the court. Such a vicious cycle may turn into a slump that will last as long as the player is unaware of the inner sources of his depression.

Your mind-body integration potential

Perhaps the most difficult part of tennis is coming to grips with your physical, intellectual, and emotional limitations. Tennis is a demanding game, and it's not hard to come up with good excuses when mind-body integration fails. You may complain that you're out of shape, worried about the kids, or distracted by business problems. These are typical rationalizations that tennis players use to avoid the emotional pain of acknowledging defects in their game. But such rationalizations can only keep you from improving your game, because they cloud your awareness of the emotions that have interfered with your play. If you give in to excuses, you will be unable to form a clear picture of your potential capacities.

Athletic ability and top physical condition are necessary for good tennis, but raising your game to the Total Tennis level requires intellectual and emotional mastery. Tennis is a mind-body game in the sense that the body's performance always reflects the player's state of mind. You can always improve your game by working with your intellect and paying attention to your emotions.

Tennis is primarily a game of techniques and strategies that require a spontaneous, "automatic" excellence in stroke execution. You can achieve this excellence if your mind is working with your body on the court. By becoming aware of how your aggressive, sexual, and narcissistic tensions influence your performance, you can control the dynamic interplay between body, intellect, and emotion. Being *aware* gives you the potential for change in the right direction.

·3·

Learning Tennis

The best tennis players know that you're not through with learning tennis when you've grasped the fundamentals of strokes and strategy. What you must do is keep learning. If you stop learning, your game will become static. But what is learning, and how do you learn? If you feel you've stopped learning, how can you get started again?

In sports, learning is intellectual, emotional, and physical; it is stimulated by repetition and imitation. Moreover, it cannot occur when the learning channels are blocked by emotional problems. In other words, your learning capacity in tennis depends on your mind-body integration.

One of the best ways to learn is by repetition, setting down memory traces in the mind and body so that each time an action is repeated, the concept becomes better understood and the skill becomes better executed. As children, we learn to walk by repeated effort; in tennis, we perfect a stroke by drilling over and over. Repetition is the most direct method for teaching the body to act, and therefore it can be thought of as the primary stimulation to physical learning. But if you have ever practice-repeated anything intensely—from piano to typing to tennis strokes—you know that repetition by itself does not produce learning. It must be accompanied by motivation. Without motivation, repetition can become a forced mechanical effort that dulls learning. Bill Tilden could have practiced his backhand for ten years to no avail if he had not been properly motivated. It was his strong motivation that enabled him to use repetition to stimulate learning.

As you drill a stroke, notice whether and how the repetition is helping you to learn. Notice how you *feel* about the stroke and about the repetition itself. Are you experiencing it positively, as a push to action, or does it make you feel a little depressed and tense? If you don't feel alert and positive during the drill, it's unlikely that you'll learn anything from it.

If you have your emotions under control, repeated practice can help you work effectively with the component movements that lead to good stroke production. Through repetition you can establish checkpoints for examining unforced errors. For proper weight transfer on your forehand drive, do you need to exaggerate the positioning of your back foot, or do you do it right spontaneously? One player who didn't bend his knee enough for low forehands found a solution by saying to himself, "Take a *big* step" (which required bending the knee). By repeating this over and over, he crystallized the stroke so that bending his left knee for low forehands became automatic. Another player could not keep her elbow down on her backhand until she imagined herself scraping the court surface with the racquet head each time she practiced bringing her racquet back.

Imitation is the second basic learning method. Imitative learning begins with the child making the sounds he hears his parents make, so that he can learn to talk to express his needs. It continues in childhood as a brother watches his older sister hold a fork or tie a shoelace. Imitation is simply copying the actions of others, but imitative *learning* is different—it implies that we gain understanding and proficiency from the experience of imitating. And the result of imitative learning is always original, because each person is selective in what he imitates and how he imitates; thus, we impose our individuality on what we learn. This is why a child's accent is always unique; although it strongly reflects his environment and his parents' accent, it's different in some ways because the child's mind selects and organizes what he imitates. So don't be afraid of plagiarizing someone's forehand; if you learn anything at all from the imitation, the stroke will develop into a forehand that's genuinely yours.

In tennis we emulate our heroes. Twenty years ago only a handful of players hit the two-handed backhand; now it's as popular as the one-hander. Why? Despite the many articles about the pros and cons of the two-handed versus the one-handed backhand, it's not the consideration of backhand mechanics that mainly determines our choice of backhand. It's our tendency to identify with our heroes—and today Evert Lloyd, Austin, Borg, and Connors all use the two-hander. There are, of course, other reasons for choosing a stroke, but identification with and imitation of contemporary heroes has a lot to do with it.

Imitation also has its dangers. If you imitate without paying attention to your thoughts and feelings in making a stroke, you may be simulating a Jack Kramer forehand but you may also be making more than your share of unforced errors. The classic flat forehand drive may not be the stroke for you. Always be sure you are *learning* from imitation, rather than just imitating.

Repetition and imitation are modes for learning, but real learning in tennis occurs only when the mind and body make the necessary connections physiologically, intellectually, and emotionally. Repeated practice of the forehand volley with a ball machine can lead to learning if it doesn't bore you. And when you're doing an "imitation drill"—imitating your favorite pro—your body will learn from the experience if you feel good enough about both yourself and the person whose stroke you're imitating. But if imitation and repeated practice bore and exhaust you, it may be because your suppressed emotional tensions are interfering with your mind-body integration. The sheer aggression of hitting an overhead smash may touch off emotionally hot attitudes in you about hostility and domination. You could react by pushing yourself all the more, ignoring the emotional attitudes that may be interfering with your play. Or you could react by not practicing certain strokes because they disturb or bore you. But without practice, you don't acquire skill. The only way to become skilled in a problem area is to confront the emotions that are blocking your skill.

Teaching Methods

Even if you have never thought about the different kinds of teaching and learning methods, your learning style and experiences in tennis will have led you to some form of "tennis philosophy" that helps guide your practice and performance. As you deal with your learning problems, especially if you are taking tennis lessons, it will help you to consider the different teaching methods, decide what you like or dislike about each of them, and experiment with them. There are many teaching methods in vogue, and you will find that each method can be classified according to which of the three aspects of mind-body integration it emphasizes: body, intellect, or emotion. *Body* teaching trains players in the mechanics of stroke production, footwork, body conditioning, calisthenics, drills, and intensive practice, helping the player improve physical coordination, agility, speed, strength, and endurance. *Intellect* teaching emphasizes using the rational and logical faculties of the mind to achieve mastery through tactics and strategy. And *emotional self-awareness* teaching often comes close to Yoga and Zen ideas, stressing the influence of internal conflicts on learning and performance.

As you look at the teaching methods you have encountered, you'll probably notice that they emphasize one aspect of mind-body integration but also touch on the other two aspects. The least effective teaching methods are those that deal with *only* the body, *only* the intellect, or *only* the emotions. The better the teaching method, the closer it will come to taking into account all three aspects of mind-body integration. Let's take a look at the three basic kinds of teaching method and examples of how they are represented in the teachings of Dennis Van der Meer, Chet Murphy, and Timothy Gallwey.

Body Teaching

Body-teaching systems view the tennis player as a primarily physical phenomenon whose task is to learn the mechanics of stroke production and to drill to improve reflexes for better footwork and accurate passing shots. The principles of body teaching are best summed up in Dennis Van der Meer's progression-checkpoint method, a pragmatic approach based on an objective assessment of the player's physical strengths and weaknesses. Van der Meer believes that the teacher's primary task is to teach the component parts of each stroke so that the player can learn stroke "units" easily and later integrate the units into whole strokes. As his body learns the parts of each stroke, the player develops checkpoints to correct unforced errors, and as he progresses at his own pace to a higher level of learning he "breaks down" and "builds up" strokes. Repetition and imitation are two central learning features in this method, and they are used to reinforce understanding of the mechanics of stroke production. The student learns to analyze what is behind persistent body problems like sloppy footwork or poor racquet control. For example, if he repeatedly hooks his forehand drive instead of firmly hitting through, he learns to use checkpoints to understand why he is not positioning himself properly. In this way he explores the limits of his physical abilities and develops a feel for strokes. In the Van der Meer method the teacher observes, identifies problems in stroke production and body movement, and recommends corrective measures. Van der Meer assumes that the body cannot learn physical skills without training, and so he breaks down complex tennis strokes to manageable units that are easier for the student to grasp. He uses a video recorder to help the student see and compare the deficient and the corrected strokes.

Over the years Van der Meer has modified his body-oriented method into a more eclectic approach, taking into account various emotional and intellectual factors. This is a logical development, because Van der Meer is primarily interested in results, and he has found that emotional awareness and intellectual understanding facilitate high-level results. He has thus developed his method beyond the purely physical. He is attracted to any idea that will bring results, and is therefore open to every theory, from Vic Braden's ideas on biological and mechanical phenomena to Jaroslav Houba's graduated length method. The eclectic nature of Van der Meer's method makes it effective and useful in many cases, but it is not complete.

In my opinion, Van der Meer's approach makes teaching

tennis too one-sided, with the teacher-technician demonstrating the mechanics of stroke production, and the student observing and imitating. Although Van der Meer individualizes his approach according to the particular student's needs, he still does not pay enough attention to the *emotional and intellectual* aspects of learning. The result can be good form without skill, rote learning rather than ꞁnderstanding. Van der Meer's goal—teaching proper technique for effective stroke production—is a good one, but it bypasses the student's *experience* of technique, and his personal conflicts and inhibitions about performance. The experience of technique leads to learning only when the student has confidence in his body's ability to learn. If the student does not have this confidence, the Van der Meer method may leave him with a good set of rules to follow, but without the solid emotional base necessary for him to achieve reliable stroke production. Only through a personalized teacher-student alliance can the teacher guide the student toward the delicate balance of spontaneity and automatic functioning necessary for skillful play.

Van der Meer's method is what it claims to be. A player with a particular mechanical problem, like a hitch in his serve, can be helped by a Van der Meer–style teacher who will figure out what the mechanical problem is and come up with useful solutions. For instance, if a beginning player has a droopy elbow, Van der Meer may recommend pointing the elbow at the ball during the toss—sound mechanical advice. His correction methods are thorough; Van der Meer insists that students review the basics of a problem stroke until they have a comprehensive understanding of the mechanical problem. He uses instant video replay to allow students to see their strokes for the first time. And he offers analogies that can help (like "hitting up on the serve with a karate motion"). The method works well as a corrective measure; perhaps Van der Meer's approach works best in helping the player to get his body to do something it could not do before. But the method does not deal with the personality and emotions of the student or the complex learning process of each individual. It's pure body integration, and it works only if you already have your intellect and emotions working together and in harmony with your body.

Intellect Teaching

If you are serious about tennis, you have probably had the experience of thinking about your body very objectively, as if it were a biological machine, and trying to figure out how to operate the machine at top efficiency. You may have practiced shortening your backswing to return fast first serves. When you do this, you are using an intellectual approach to tennis—seeing the player (yourself) as a physical phenomenon and using your brain to decide how to use your body.

Intellect teaching combines game plans, court tactics, percentage tennis concepts, and scientific research, to arrive at a new philosophy that often runs counter to classical ideas about tennis form. One of the top proponents of intellect teaching systems is Chet Murphy, an expert on the mechanics and aerodynamics of tennis. He views good form as a science to be learned by applying the principles of physics to stroke production and body movement. On the basis of extensive studies of form and movement—including the use of picture-frame analysis of stroke production—Murphy advocates radical changes in teaching tennis. He wants to make strokes and body movements relevant to the demands of the game situation, rather than let abstract concepts of form predetermine the limits of play. Classical form *per se* is of no use to Murphy; he's interested in what works. If a stroke works, he finds out why it works and how to use it.

He sees the moving body as a system of levers. The arm—along with its extension, the racquet—is the principal lever because it makes the final movement that sends the ball on its way. The legs act as levers to get the body into position to hit the ball correctly. In Murphy's view, understanding how your body parts work as levers will help you to consolidate your intuitive grasp of tennis, and will thus improve your strokes and timing. In a sense it is intellect-body integration.

Murphy believes that good form is relative to the task at hand. He teaches many strokes to cover different court contingencies, basing each stroke on sound mechanical and aerodynamic principles. When he instructs a player, he asks if the stroke is working, and if not, why not. When a stroke doesn't work for a court situation, he will look for another stroke that will work. Thus, in teaching volleys, he goes beyond conventional teaching of the block and punch volleys and recommends strokes based on logical analysis of the shot sequence. He recommends following your serve with a cross-court drive volley when the conventional punch volley won't work because you are not close enough into the net. Many players with fast first serves do this intuitively; John Newcombe perfected this shot because he realized that he couldn't maintain the initiative with the punch volley.

Murphy's teaching suggests a logical approach to shot selection that varies according to the particular player's physical limitations. Each stroke has indications and contraindications. Technical measures for the stroke vary with flight of the ball, location of the opponent, and mechanics. Strokes are judged by their effectiveness.

Murphy's ideas are revolutionizing contemporary concepts of good form on the tennis court. Top coaches are demonstrating that what happens at the moment of impact determines the effectiveness of a stroke, and that ball placement depends on the angle of deflection or the angle of incidence at impact. It's an objective, scientific approach. According to Murphy, good form has three outstanding characteristics: the motion is economical; the component parts of the stroke are harmonious; and, above all, *the total form is efficient in getting the job done.*

Chet Murphy's teaching methods provide a scientific approach to help the tennis player understand the mechanical and aerodynamic principles behind efficient stroke production. His research data clarify the relationship between form and the hit; he teaches students to modify form for efficient shot-making. His plea for flexible tennis instruction is intended to make the tennis player an active participant in his own learning.

Teaching more strokes to cover different court contingencies can help the player master difficulties in actual play. But some people claim that scientific understanding and larger stroke repertoires interfere with learning. These "anti-intellectual" players say that learning more about strokes only makes things worse, crowding the mind with information and choices that interfere with spontaneous play. Many of the world's leading players, they say, don't know what a lever is and have no interest in the physics of tennis.

This viewpoint does not take into account the value of understanding the logic of stroke production. Intellect teaching can take the player to new levels of intellect-body integration by focusing attention on how the body is challenged. It is especially relevant for the pressures of competition.

Bjorn Borg's forehand scoop stroke is an interesting example of using intellect in a strategy that counters the body's limitations. When faced with a deep, hard-hit ball that he can barely reach with his forehand, Bjorn relies on a scooping motion to gain topspin, height, and depth. By using the opponent's pace and a lot of wrist, he takes into account both mechanical and aerodynamic problems. His stroke is remarkably effective since the opponent often can't reach the ball, and its spin keeps it safely inside the court.

It's easy to confuse body and emotional learning. Using intellect to compensate for what the body can't do works only if the player's main problem is a body problem. When the problem is an emotionally based learning block, then intellectual focus *does* distract. That's when an emotional focus is needed.

A college professor who was having trouble with his overhead smash decided to make a study of the stroke in order to master it. He read books, gathered information, took lessons, and drilled. But learning more only made things worse—he couldn't put it all together. Finally, when he saw that his intellectual approach wasn't working, he decided that there must be something emotional to his problem. He continued to practice, but started to focus on the emotional tensions he experienced as he tried to hit the overhead. In doing this, he realized that the actual thought of the overhead made him nervous; he caught himself feeling afraid that he would hurt his opponent or split the ball in two. His fears were causing him to hesitate, and this ruined the timing of his stroke.

He thought about this during and after matches, and tried to figure out why he should be so afraid of hitting the ball too hard, why he should worry about hurting someone by being too aggressive. A lot of childhood memories came back to him, and he began to get a feeling for why he was holding back emotionally in his tennis game.

After three or four weeks of this introspection, he began to notice that he was less anxious on the court when the time came for him to make an overhead smash. Slowly his stroke improved. He had had an emotional breakthrough, and was now able to use the intellectual knowlege he had acquired in his reading and lessons.

Intellectual learning in tennis should not be undervalued, but we must realize that it has value only when the player has worked through his problem spots with emotional awareness.

Emotional Self-Awareness Teaching

Many tennis teachers wince when they see a player tighten up, forget everything he has been taught, and drive the ball into the net. Coordinated, smooth functioning has been destroyed by inner tensions. Although the teacher may see this happening in his student, telling the student "You're too tense" rarely solves anything. The teacher may think, "If I could only get this guy interested in hitting the ball right rather than winning every point, then maybe he'd relax long enough to give his body a chance to perform." Smooth, coordinated functioning, the hallmark of every great athlete, occurs when the player has a self-confident attitude about his talent and ability. How can a teacher or coach foster this ability? How can the player's self-critical attitude and competitive conflicts be dealt with by the teacher? Classical teaching methods like "Back to the basics" may only make the player more uptight, as he tries to concentrate harder to do what he knows. Tennis can be an extremely frustrating game for the player who can't get his body to do what it's been learning for years to do.

To respond to these practical problems, many tennis teachers have recently been experimenting with Yoga and Zen ideas, psychological relaxation techniques (including hypnosis), and sensitivity methods that increase the player's self-awareness so that he can relax on the court and use his potential more effectively.

Timothy Gallwey's books (*The Inner Game of Tennis* and *Inner Tennis: A Practical Guide*, both published by Random House) have helped many frustrated players to do this. Gallwey has encouraged students to trust their feelings and experiences and to make them the focal point of learning. His inner-game approach asserts that the body has a natural way of learning physical skills. Trust your feelings; believe that your body will find *its* way—that's the Gallwey message. Unlike Van der Meer, Gallwey believes that the body does not need to be trained. He encourages the beginning player to relax his will and let his body function. To do this, the player must be able to dominate the part of his mind that judges, criticizes, approves, or disapproves. When the player can stop worrying about winning, view his experience as part of a developmental process in learning about himself, and trust his integrative functions, then total stroke (gestalt) learning can occur.

Gallwey's method is directed at the stresses that interfere with learning and performance. He asks the player to think about his inner emotional life, to recognize the conflict between Self 1 (the critical mind) and Self 2 (the part of the mind that registers body experiences). Gallwey's method uses exercises designed to promote emotional self-awareness and self-discipline. When Self 2 dominates Self 1 so that body and mind are not in conflict, then useful, noncritical self-observing can occur, providing the mind with the information it needs to improve body functioning. Gallwey opposes intellect teaching, contending that rational analysis of strokes interferes with the mind's experiencing and self-observing functions, with feeling and seeing. According to Gallwey, the player's learning task is to produce the emotional conditions that will help the body to perform well.

Gallwey says that the battle between Self 1 and Self 2 is more important than the competition between you and your opponent. In the Inner Game philosophy, winning is not the main goal, but a side effect of a calm mind that permits optimal bodily functioning. The Gallway method aims at eliminating the inner obstacles to performance so that the player can use his full potential. He says that when this occurs, Self 1 and Self 2 merge into an egoless identity and the true self emerges.

Gallwey is primarily interested in learning—what helps it and what interferes with it. He writes, "I didn't one day stop teaching the outer game and start teaching the Inner Game; I started getting interested in learning."[1] He advocates tennis pros identifying in spirit with judo masters rather than with teaching technicians. He believes that the tennis teacher can introduce people to self-knowledge rather than simply teach the mechanics of strokes.

In Gallwey's view, learning comes from within the student; the instructor's role is to provide a learning experience. Praise, positive reinforcement, and criticism are avoided because they distract from the inner-game motif of learning about yourself. Like Murphy, but for different reasons, Gallwey is against the overemphasis on form that characterizes so much of current tennis instruction. Gallway wants to promote *feel* rather than form. The student who becomes preoccupied with the proper form of his strokes or how his game looks to others loses touch with his inner experience. Gallwey says of his own learning experiences in tennis, "I was always too busy trying to do something 'right' to really feel what my body was doing."[2] When he was thirty-three years old, an instructor in hatha-yoga encouraged him to become aware of the physical sensations of his body movement. Self-experiencing helped Gallwey learn proper form quickly, and he soon decided to apply this approach to teaching tennis, and he now trains other teachers how to focus on the student's self-experiencing.

Gallwey's teaching methods represent a serious attempt to incorporate the psychology of learning into tennis teaching methods. He recognizes the importance of the player's self-image in learning tennis, drawing largely on his own experiences as an outstanding junior player and a student of hatha-yoga and Zen philosophy. He emphasizes the role of the player's self-experience in learning and teaches the player how to work with rather than against his body. Gallwey tries to eliminate self-critical attitudes by asking the player to pay more attention to self-observation and less attention to goals. If you ignore the competitive factor in tennis, if you suppress your impulse to say "sorry" to your doubles partner, then, says Gallwey, you can concentrate on your sensations, thoughts, feelings, and kinesthetic experiences; you can dominate Self 1 and realize your inner potentials for improved play.

Gallwey's teaching philoscphy has stirred intense controversy and confusion among tennis teachers. Some feel that it's a fallacious method offering an easy way out for players who don't want to practice; others say it's a cult that requires almost religious adherence to get any results. What about these criticisms?

First of all, Gallwey's system is not an easy way out, although it sometimes attracts people who think it is. Emotional learning is no easier than learning the basics, but it's a different kind of learning. When Gallwey's method is used correctly, it can bring about important emotional integrations that do improve play.

The real problem is that Gallwey underrates the roles of intellectual and physical learning. The student who is in control of his emotions, but has no solid base of practice and strategic understanding, is out in the cold when it's time to deal with the realities of tennis. This is why Gladys Heldman observes that Gallwey's followers "are still missing the same kinds of shots and still losing to the same kinds of players."[3]

Is the Gallwey method too cultist? Do you need a guru to

do it right? It's true that any self-improvement system takes dedication. But Gallwey's system demands more than that. Barbara Breit Gordon, an experienced tennis teacher who combines Gallwey's method with other techniques, thinks that the method itself is not successful—it's the belief in it that can help. Some believe that it will work only if you believe in Zen or overidealize Gallwey himself. This is fine, but it means that the method will work only for a limited number of students.

Gallwey's techniques help players who suffer from psychological problems affecting their body image and interfering with spontaneous physical reactions—players who have self-critical, self-defeating attitudes although they do not suffer too deeply from these attitudes. The Gallwey method provides for the student an almost hypnotic means of getting around these attitudes and achieving spontaneity. It is true, as Gallwey maintains, that too much worrying about performance will interfere with your game; it is true that you should let your body move naturally. But this does not provide the crucial breakthrough needed by the majority of tennis players. Gallwey's method lacks an in-depth understanding of individual motivations and conflicts about mastery and competition, and therefore it provides solutions only for those players who have already identified their motivations and conflicts.

The Learning Alliance

The intellectual and emotional interplay between teacher and student is the foundation of the learning process. We cannot make ourselves learn, but we can establish optimal conditions under which the mind can make the connections necessary for learning. The most important of these conditions is the learning alliance—the relationship between teacher and student.

Whether you take lessons or learn to play with a teaching pro, a friend, or family member, the formation of a learning alliance is the first step toward learning. Why is it important? Because we learn from *people*, and how we feel about them determines how well we learn from them. The learning alliance provides the matrix for learning and is based on mutual trust, confidence, and respect.

Whatever the teacher's philosophy, he must adjust his methods to the needs of the student—needs that he will be aware of via his personal relationship with the student. Every student has a different set of emotional needs that have to be satisfied if he is to learn, and the good teacher will sense what these needs are and how to work with them to provide a good learning experience. This means that the teacher has to be more than just a top tennis player—he must be psychologically intuitive and be able to establish rapport between himself and the student. He has to have some sense of how the student *feels* about a two-handed backhand in order to find out why the student is having trouble with it. The teaching pro is there not just to teach stroke mechanics (though that's part of it), but to teach the student how to feel confident about the stroke. He does this by guiding the student toward perceptions that further mind-body integration and by helping him to reinforce these perceptions with checkpoints.

The good teaching pro is an objective observer, pointing out strengths and weaknesses that the student may miss in himself. More important, the good pro is able to help the student gradually make self-observation a part of his playing style. In other words, the pro fulfills certain functions; he should be able to teach the student to take over these functions and incorporate them into his playing. The teaching pro also has to figure out (and communicate) not only the capabilities of his student, but also what can be anticipated by and from the opponent.

To be able to do these things, the teaching pro must himself be an emotionally aware person—aware not only of his student's emotions, but also of his own feelings. He must be able to feel and understand his own anxieties and tensions in order to help his student acknowledge and tolerate similar feelings. How does the pro feel about the frustration of losing? If he has not worked out his own frustrations, he won't be able to empathize with a student whose learning process is impeded by frustration. And if he doesn't empathize with the student, the student will not be able to open up about his frustration and get to the bottom of it; mind-body integration channels will be blocked.

The learning alliance is above all a two-way process; the student must take an active part in his own learning experience. At the core of the learning alliance is trust. No matter how good the teaching pro is, if you do not completely trust him on a personal level, you will learn little. Trust is a tricky emotion; it may be that the teacher is very trustworthy, but the student is unable to form the bond of trust. The inability to trust others usually originates in childhood disappointment with parents or teachers who were once idealized; in conflicts with sadistic, narcissistic, or seductive authority figures; or in the inability to trust oneself. Lack of trust can disrupt the learning alliance before it gets started. Players who can't trust others usually have difficulty with tennis lessons. Those who have a strong need to do things their way may worry that a teaching pro will try to change their game. Those who are afraid of being manipulated and controlled may feel that lessons take the fun out of tennis.

Examine your ability to place trust in others. If you have had bad childhood experiences in trusting parents or teachers; if you are unconsciously afraid of being controlled because of your experiences with a domineering parent; or if you generally find it difficult to place trust in authority figures, then ask yourself if your lack of trust in the teaching pro originates in your inability to totally trust anyone. If you feel this is what's happening, try to overcome your distrust by talking to the teaching pro about it. One of the big factors in the learning alliance is the ability of student and teacher to talk with each other about emotional apprehensions as well as aims and ambitions.

John, a seventeen-year-old high-school junior, had taken lessons for two years with a teaching pro. They had a good relationship based on John's admiration of the pro's skill and warmth, and the pro's recognition that John was serious about tennis. John did a lot of imitative learning, modeling his service motion, ball toss, and snap of the wrist on his image of the pro's serve.

John's interest in tennis had begun with his identification with his uncle, a locally ranked player. A good deal of his motivation had always been his wish to play at his uncle's level. Finally, when his uncle realized that John was getting good, he invited John to play a set. This was exciting; John felt that he still wasn't good enough to beat his uncle, but he was anxious to show off his serve and see if he could ace his uncle a few times.

The game was a disaster. John won the toss and elected to serve, powering his first serve deeply into his uncle's forehand side, and his uncle netted the serve return. But after that it was all downhill. John's timing on his service motion went wrong, and got worse with frustration. His toss became inconsistent, and he lost the snap in his serve. His uncle won 6-0. "What happened?" John asked his teaching pro after the set. "It was like I was a beginner. You name it, I did it wrong! I forgot everything I'd ever learned about the game."

John's pro simply smiled and said, "Okay, let's get back to the drawing board and find out what happened." As they practiced together, the pro was reassured that John's serve was technically sound, and that there wasn't any real mechanical reason why he should have bombed out so completely. This set him to thinking about whether John's relationship with his uncle had set the psychological stage for failure. At the next lesson he asked John if he had had any more ideas about the game. "Something must have been wrong in my head," John moaned. "I won that first point, and then something just happened." "That's the point," said the pro, adding, "What was it that happened?—and did it happen *because* you won that first point?"

John and his pro then launched into a half-hour discussion of why John's performance had crumbled, and they came to the conclusion that it was because of an emotional problem rather than lack of practice or tactical understanding. It turned out that John had an intense wish to defeat his uncle on the court, and at the same time he found the whole idea frightening because he feared losing his uncle's love if he beat him. All the conflicts behind John's feelings toward his uncle had coalesced to destroy his mind-body integration.

John's good fortune at having a psychologically intuitive teacher helped a lot. But just as important was the trust and rapport that enabled them to dig into the emotional problem that had interfered with his game.

Another important aspect of the learning alliance is that it must be tuned into the player's motivation to learn. The first thing the good pro finds out is what the student wants to learn, and *why*. The pro who understands the student's motivation can deepen his rapport with the student and guide him to an emotional integration that can have a lasting effect on the student's game. Behind a player's problems with a kink in his service motion or inconsistency with his down-the-line passing shots may be a learning inhibition because these strokes have conflictual meanings for the player. If he can probe his motivation enough to find out that making the passing shot represents for him the realization of a primitive wish to prove his worth, then he can get some mileage with the stroke. By knowing the tensions involved, he can work more productively to keep them from interfering with his integration. The teaching pro who looks for the motives behind the student's wish to learn can help the student face the emotional meanings of these motives, and the consequences of their meanings for the student.

Assessing the student's motivation is one of the more difficult tasks the teaching pro faces. Many players, especially juniors, are shy about expressing their motives and fears about learning tennis, which then need to be drawn out by the pro. If the pro fails to clarify the student's motives, then the learning alliance may falter.

Motivation is not a static attribute that the tennis player carries into the learning alliance. The alliance itself can contribute to the student's motivation, especially when the teacher serves as an ego-ideal figure for the student. The teaching pro, with his skill and knowledge of the game, is

cast in a superior role and most students, if only unconsciously, look up to him and idealize him, as children idealize their
parents. A good teaching pro evokes in his students the motivation to play better because they want to please him, whether they realize it or not. This happened in our example of
John who modeled his game after his pro's, and improved his
play through imitative learning.

Just as a good learning alliance can motivate the student,
a poor alliance can destroy his interest. The teacher may not
understand enough about the player's tennis ambitions or secret fears.

> Eva, a fine player in her early teens, had a secret ambition to
> develop the big game with a cannonball serve like Arthur
> Ashe's. When the teacher showed her how to hit a spin serve,
> she became bored. All she could think about was the cannon-
> ball serve, but she felt shy about telling this to the teacher; she
> was afraid he would laugh at her for overrating her abilities.
> Not surprisingly, she dropped out of the lesson program after a
> few weeks, rationalizing that her school grades might suffer be-
> cause tennis was taking too much of her time. The real reason
> was that Eva had lost her motivation because the teaching alli-
> ance had not been conducive to her expressing her goals and
> her anxieties about her abilities.

In a good learning alliance the student can discuss his ambitions and fears with the teacher, because the teacher is receptive and encourages the student to express his anxieties.
Even when a student is grandiose and sets unrealistic goals,
the sensitive pro will be patient, work with the student, and
help the student gradually form a realistic picture of his
abilities, rather than deflate the student's ego with put-
downs. This is one of the tests of a good pro, because many
teachers find it impossible to put up with cocky, grandiose
students who think they know everything there is to know
about tennis. The good pro can control his natural reaction to
such arrogance—he knows that sometimes these students *are*
fine players. And conversely, he recognizes that many shy
players have secret grandiose ambitions, and that these ambitions can motivate the student to learn.

In the best learning alliances, the teacher assumes roles that help the student to work with his learning problems— roles that may vary from parent to friend to instructor to something close to a psychiatrist. The good teacher knows how to find a player's potential even when it's covered up by emotional, physical, or mind-body integration problems. When he works with an adolescent who is in the middle of an awkward growth spurt, the good pro recognizes that concentration and coordination problems can't be instructed away by telling the junior to move his feet and keep his eye on the ball. By remembering the awkwardness he experienced in his own adolescence, he is more likely to figure out a way to work around these problems. He may find it necessary to use drills that accentuate the adolescent's strong points, to build up his confidence. He will be sensitive to the physical and emotional stress points of his students, whether they are adolescents or executives.

A young mother who had never played tennis before decided to take lessons, mainly to get back into shape after having a baby. She had been inspired by reading about Evonne Goolagong's comeback after her pregnancy. When the pro met the player for her first lesson, he asked her why she was interested in tennis, and she said, "Oh, just to get some exercise and do a little social playing. I don't want to set the world on fire. I'm not really that good an athlete—I avoided sports in school."

The pro began working on hand-eye coordination with a racquet and ball, and then decided to teach volleying to help her consolidate her racquet control. He planned his lessons carefully to build up her confidence, because he sensed that she felt vulnerable to criticism. After half a dozen lessons she graduated to ground strokes. The pro felt he had dealt with her apprehension, but because she seemed to be holding back a little, he began to wonder if she was getting what she wanted from her lessons. He asked her how she felt about them and if she wanted to go in a different direction. She answered that she was liking tennis more than she thought she would, and was thinking about having two lessons a week. She told the pro that she hated to do things unless she got really involved. The pro realized that she was contradicting what she had first told him about how superficial her interest in tennis was. What was her real motivation, and how could he use it to help her to play well?

As she moved into two lessons a week, the pro gained more insight into her motivation. Although she was learning quickly, she would always pick on herself for her weak points and joke about being awkward. Finally, the pro decided to talk to her about her motivation. He reviewed the lesson program they had undertaken. In discussing her interest in Evonne Goolagong the pro asked what it was about Goolagong that she admired most. Without thinking she blurted out, "Her freedom." Goolagong's natural coordination and ease was what appealed to her most. When the pro pointed out how self-critical she was, she wondered about this since she had not paid much attention to the way she attacked herself on the court.

This conversation was the turning point in the young mother's learning. The pro helped her uncover her true motivation—to play a sport without judging herself harshly, and to enjoy playing. Like so many players who are afraid of failure or of embarrassing themselves, she had initially held back in her efforts because she was afraid she wouldn't get what she wanted from tennis.

Every player approaches lessons with his own ambitions and fears. Many juniors secretly hope they are talented and that the teacher will take a special interest in their progress. They often have grandiose ambitions or wish to learn a difficult stroke, like the American twist serve, without first mastering the basics. Older players may harbor similar ambitions, but they often feel embarrassed to talk freely about their tennis fantasies and fears, especially if they are worried about getting hurt or overexerting themselves.

No matter what age the student, all these feelings need to be acknowledged and shared with the pro. In a good learning alliance, emotional honesty between student and teacher facilitates the rapport and collaborative effort necessary for learning. Mutual trust leads to a free interchange of viewpoints and objective criticism, and the student gains valuable experience in managing his feelings in an interpersonal relationship. In a well-developed learning alliance, the student can identify and express his frustrations with the practical application of lessons, and the good pro will anticipate the student's frustrations and prepare him to cope with the problems that stand in the way of mastery. As the student learns, his confidence increases; when problems arise, he is able to rely on what he has been taught. Genuine self-reliance—essential for learning and mastering tennis—can be achieved only when the player is able to identify and work with the emotional tensions that cause mind-body integration failures. A one-to-one relationship with the right teaching pro can help you to work with your emotions toward the goal of mastery.

Students who can't or won't discuss their ambitions and fears with their teacher usually become discouraged with lessons. They may bemoan the gap between what they have been taught and the realities of competitive play, rather than face the communication gap in the learning alliance. These students have trouble achieving enough self-confidence to learn and master tennis. In the stress of competition, when their ambitions and fears are exposed, they often forget what they have been taught and lose confidence in their game.

Jimmy Connors is the foremost example of a top player who has genuine self-confidence based on a learning alliance that produced trust. No matter what the result, Jimmy repeats time and again, "I always play the same—*I play the way I was taught*" (author's italics). And he often adds, "Usually that's good enough to win."

Self-confidence is an extremely important factor in the learning alliance because it reflects the student's capacity to regulate his inner tensions and trust in his ability to function effectively. Connors's confidence is reinforced not only by his success in tournament competition but also by his inner psychological experience every time he hits a well-grooved, rippling, deep ground stroke. He is one of the best-coached players in tennis today and undoubtedly much of his confidence stems from his having been trained by his mother and by the renowned Pancho Segura. Connors exemplifies how innate self-assurance can be reinforced by a learning alliance based on mutual trust and good rapport.

A good learning alliance, then, requires mutual trust, rapport, and understanding. If both student and teacher understand the player's motivations, the teaching pro can offer objective criticism to the student in a way that promotes learning. The basic aim of the learning alliance is to establish a learning process that takes into account the player's talent, motivation, physical capacity, ambitions and fears, and potential learning problems. The bottom-line question is, "Is this player learning at an optimal pace to bring out his potential capacity, motivation, and ability?"

Problems in the Learning Alliance

Unfortunately, a great deal can go wrong in the relationship between teacher and student. We have discussed the most common problem in learning—the failure to form a learning alliance. The player who is untrusting, poorly motivated, or too worried about failure may not be able to enter into an alliance with a teaching pro. For some players, frustrations, competitive anxieties, or self-esteem problems may interfere with the learning alliance. Or the player may form an unrealistic attachment to the teacher, attributing powers to him that exist only in fantasy. Overidealization of teachers, or romantic fantasies, can motivate the player to improve in order to please the teacher. But if a teacher makes the mistake of openly favoring one student or a group of players, then the learning alliance can be destroyed by jealousy and rivalry among the students. Or the teaching pro may lose interest in teaching due to frustration, long working hours, or professional or personal conflicts about teaching. If the teacher himself has lost interest, we cannot expect him to be able to motivate his students or to maintain any kind of learning alliance.

Many times it's hard to put your finger on exactly what is wrong with a learning alliance. If you're not learning, you have to assume that either you have a learning block or there is a problem with the learning alliance. The problems that can come up in a learning alliance are simply human-relationship problems likely to arise between two people in a teaching/learning situation. Such problems usually show up in the following essential areas:

—Trusting others

—Identifying with others

—Empathizing with others (understanding how they feel)

—Expressing your feelings

—Allowing others to express their feelings

—Seeing people as they are in reality, rather than as they seem to be because of your unconscious fantasies and idealizations

There is only one sure way to find out what kind of problem you have (learning block or alliance), and that is to examine and identify the tensions that you feel, and try to find the tensions that you suppress.

When you are having trouble learning and playing you should be able to identify your tensions as belonging to either a bored or an overexcited emotional state.

Boredom is usually experienced in the following ways, all of which disrupt the learning process:

—Subtle failures in concentration, such as the inability to keep your eye on the ball or follow the game plan

—Listless attitude that keeps you from hustling on difficult points

—Indifference to learning and playing

—Restlessness that goes from one learning goal to another as your mind flits back and forth from solution to solution with no sustained focus

—Self-absorbed preoccupations that you keep trying to push out of your mind

—Emotional fatigue along with an inability to mobilize your physical energies

—An altered sense of time, so that a lesson or a tennis match seems to drag on and on

Boredom is the mind's way of signaling that emotional tension is being suppressed. The bored player feels listless and tired and avoids facing his emotional tension by adopting an indifferent attitude about learning and playing. He shrugs off his poor concentration with the excuse that he's just having a bad day. But when he plays again, determined to try harder and concentrate on every point, he gets frustrated and depressed because of his failure to make progress. To escape the frustration and depression, the student suppresses his feelings and soothes himself by taking an indifferent, bored attitude. If the boredom continues and the student remains blocked in his learning, the problem can usually be traced to a psychological conflict about learning. Such conflicts can undermine the learning alliance.

One common, but usually unrecognized, cause of boredom is a student's unconscious need to thwart the teacher's efforts. This may seem like a strange idea since the student may consciously admire the teacher and value his lessons. In his conscious thinking he may be making a concerted effort to learn. But if the student unconsciously envies or resents the teacher, his unconscious conflicts will interfere with learning. He tries to learn but he can't maintain interest; in spite of his wish to learn, he makes no progress. He tries and fails over and over, each failure reinforcing his original boredom. He says to the teacher, "I see what you mean, but I can't do it." The result is that the student doesn't learn, and he unconsciously blames the teacher for having failed to teach him. For the student who unconsciously envies the teacher, learning and playing well would be an acknowledgment of the teacher's effectiveness (or, translated into sexual terms, his potency or sexual competence). The student's failure to learn or perform well is a passive way of expressing an aggressive feeling—unconscious envy of the teacher's knowledge and ability. By defeating the teacher's efforts, the student is saying, "You're not as good as you think you are—look at how badly I'm playing."

Sometimes the student's boredom is a reaction to a rigid teacher who insists that the student learn a particular method and who ignores the student's need for individualized, independent learning. Many students find it difficult to express their anger when their need to learn autonomously is frustrated, and so they suppress the anger and channel it into boredom. They make the same mistakes, seem disinterested, and fail to follow advice—thus irritating the teaching pro.

To break the frustration/boredom cycle, the teaching pro should try to recall his own learning experiences to see how they influenced his teaching. Teaching pros who resented being taught in a rigid, rule-bound manner tend to repeat the mistake with their students, and they end up with bored students who cannot learn. The teacher who is irritated by such students should use his irritation as a signal to recall his own past learning experiences so that he can empathize with the student. By helping the student deal with frustration and boredom, the teacher can rebuild the alliance and give the student a creative learning experience.

The overexcited state usually reveals itself in the following reactions and attitudes, all of which affect learning:

—Excessive sweating, heart pounding, and an inability to control your body

—A feeling of being psychologically flooded by the pressure of thoughts and feelings

—Overplaying the ball, instead of playing the way you were taught

—Impulsive decisions

Behind the tennis student's overexcited state is strong emotion that blocks mind-body integration. Often this emotion takes the form of an intense wish to be better than the teacher or better than someone who is symbolized by the teacher. The student may be flooded with anxiety and guilt because he needs to beat the teacher, yet feels that he cannot or should not do so. Usually the student is unaware of his competitive conflicts with authority figures. By overplaying the ball or making impulsive decisions on the court, he may unwittingly defeat himself and thus avoid facing the conflict about winning.

When a student consistently becomes overexcited or feels panicky on the court, he has a learning problem that can be dealt with only in a good learning alliance. The teaching pro must be able to understand the relationship between the student's need to perform well and his ambivalent feelings about the teacher. Only then can he help the student work with his intense emotions by anticipating the guilt-anxiety-panic reaction that leads to the overexcited state.

What makes us want to learn about new things? Why do some things interest us more than others? And why do some people learn some things more quickly or more deeply than others do? These are only a few of the fascinating questions one could ask about learning. We will spend the rest of this chapter on two important aspects of learning in tennis: the individual's wish to learn for his own self-expression, and the different types of psychological conflicts that can interfere with a player's learning.

Every tennis player brings to the game a long history of learning experiences. Looking at these experiences will help each player understand his reasons for wanting to learn. As children, we learn to walk, talk, read, and do arithmetic, and thus master the skills required to cope with our environment. Once we have learned the basics, our interest in learning is transformed, and we begin to want to learn for different reasons. As we develop intellectually and emotionally, the experience of learning and achievement of mastery provides a channel for expressing our aggressive, sexual, and narcissistic feelings. For small children, fantasy and play are sufficient vehicles for the expression of important emotions. But as the child grows up, his needs and emotions become far more structured and thus need a more structured framework of play for self-expression. This is why we have *games*, and the important distinction between *play* and *games* lies in the structure of games, symbolized by game rules and criteria for excellence. In games, the older child and the adult discover vehicles for expressing sexual and aggressive tensions in an ordered, structured framework.

What is it that tennis allows us to express?

First of all, as we've seen, tennis is a confrontation type of game—similar to a duel—that allows us to express direct, one-to-one aggression. Conflictive situations in daily life do not usually permit us the luxury of unleashing our hostility. Even though you and your tennis opponent may be the best of friends, you both need to simulate a situation in which you can tear each other's guts out. Since you know it's simulation, you won't get upset about it—unless something in the match stirs up some unresolved conflictual tensions that you need to work on.

The tensions that interfere with learning are the same kinds of tensions that lead to choking. But you may be particularly susceptible to these tensions when you are trying to learn something new and unfamiliar, like hitting an overhead smash. In learning such a stroke you may become inhibited because of your fantasies of losing control of the racquet or hurting your opponent with the smash. If you don't stop and confront this fantasy, it may keep you from ever learning the stroke.

Why are some people afraid they'll hurt someone with the ball, while others smash away without fear? Because each person has different aggressive conflicts; the person who's afraid to let loose has had childhood experiences that taught him to suppress his aggression; furthermore, his natural conflicts about being aggressive may have been intensified by this suppression.

The serve is another stroke that presents problems in the release of aggression. Although it has the advantage of allowing you to decide when, where, and how you are going to hit it, the serve is still difficult and complicated because its movements require precise timing in the release of aggression. As you toss the ball, you must hold your aggression in for a crucial moment, and then you must suddenly explode. Most normal people have aggressive conflicts that interfere with their serve once in a while, but if you simply cannot learn the serve, look into the feelings you have about controlling the release of your aggression.

A big element in tennis—one closely related to the aggressive aspect—is that of domination. When you want to win, you want to dominate, because part of winning is controlling the course the game takes. It is good to want to be stronger than your opponent, to want to dominate him—that's part of what tennis is all about. People who have conflicts in this sphere either back away from domination and play a passive, no-win game, or go to the other extreme and try to be overly aggressive.

Either way will get you into learning problems. The too-aggressive player can't concentrate on learning strokes because his attention is absorbed in controlling the release of his aggression. The too-timid player who suppresses his aggression usually lacks the initiative necessary for autonomous learning.

Overcoming Resistance to Autonomous Learning

No matter what your reasons for playing are, you are probably aware of your general learning patterns. Some things come easier than others for you; some things never seem to come at all. Maybe you have a natural forehand, but you just can't get the hang of the backhand volley. Or maybe you're good at the net but slow on your feet and bad at covering the court. Some things seem to be unlearnable no matter how much you practice, visualize, and try. The only way to get at these problems is to pin down the feelings or conflicts behind them. When you simply can't learn a stroke or when you spot a pattern of inexplicable mistakes in the same area, you are getting close to a natural human trait in yourself: the resistance to autonomous learning.

Autonomous learning is learning *for yourself.* It means that whatever you are learning takes on an individual meaning for you; it means that even when you are imitating Manuel Orantes's dropshot, you are making it your own, feeling it as an experience that you create for yourself. Learning usually involves shared experiences with a friend or teacher or with someone you are imitating; but learning autonomously means that you are able to integrate those experiences into your private experience of your mind and body and come out with something new—something learned. The *sine qua non* of autonomous learning is the integration of new sensations and kinesthetic experiences to achieve innovative solutions to the learning problems you encounter.

People who can't learn autonomously flounder about and never seem to individualize their tennis style. Often they have problems with dependency that stem from early experiences with parents being either unavailable or too available. These players may feel supported or encouraged by a coach but have difficulty learning from the coach. This is where a good learning alliance can help; a teaching pro should be able to detect the student's resistance to autonomous learning and respond to it. The good teaching pro in this sense is in some ways like a good parent who helps the child discover his independence and his capabilities.

There are some players who think they know it all already and can't take advice or instruction. "I can do it, leave me alone," they protest, before they even understand what you're trying to explain. This is clearly not autonomous learning; such people have plenty of initiative but no capacity for mature dependency. They can rarely follow through and integrate what they learn with their own experience because their conflicts about authority figures prevent them from really knowing what their own experience is.

The first step toward autonomous learning is trusting yourself to make your own decisions.

Jimmy was a promising junior player who seemed to take in everything he was taught by his teaching pro. But in close matches he lacked confidence, and his play took on a listless, apathetic quality. His pro wondered how he could help Jimmy play more decisively in these tense match situations. When he asked Jimmy what went through his mind when the score was close, Jimmy couldn't come up with a clear answer. "I just feel I have no control over what's going to happen," he said.

The pro suggested that Jimmy start making up his own game plans and then evaluate how they worked out. By encouraging Jimmy to take an active role in his learning, the pro hoped that Jimmy could shift from the student role and take charge.

It worked! Jimmy wrote out an elaborate game plan for his next tough match. He won in three sets 6-4, 3-6, 6-3. After the match his coach asked him how he thought the plan had helped. Jimmy replied that it gave him something to do to keep him from getting nervous. The next step the coach took was to have Jimmy evaluate his game plans critically for their strengths and weaknesses. For a while Jimmy wasn't quite sure whether the game plans were helping him on the crucial points, but he kept using them for all his tough matches. A few lessons later, when he saw his coach, Jimmy felt excited. He had caught on to what his coach had in mind. Halfway through the first set of his last match, Jimmy realized that his plan to rush the net on both his serves was not working. A few games later he figured out why—he was being passed by his opponent's backhand cross-court. As a result, he changed his game plan during the second set, even though he had won the first set 7-5. He closed out the match easily 6-2 by holding his serve and cashing in on two service breaks.

Jimmy was able to learn autonomously only when he examined the results of his game plan and figured out its strong points and its weaknesses. He put himself on the line by first deciding what he would try to do in close matches, and then evaluating how successful his plans had been.

What had stopped Jimmy from making his own decisions in the first place? Like many young players, Jimmy had a lot to learn about the game, and since his coach had always helped him to solve his stroke and footwork problems, he naturally looked to the coach for advice when things went wrong. But Jimmy's learning dependence had a deeper basis: he was afraid of embarrassing himself by being too cocky and then making a mistake—that's why he had asked his parents for tennis lessons in the first place. He also worried that, if left to his own devices, he would learn bad habits and develop poor strokes. He didn't trust his own natural learning processes.

Autonomous learning requires a balance of initiative and mature dependency. If you're a beginner it makes sense to rely on an expert to learn good stroke production, but if this reliance supplants natural curiosity and keeps you from experimenting with your own ideas, then what you learn will not be *yours*.

In searching out the reasons for your learning problems, you will eventually find out that learning and performance are intimately connected. If you have an aggressive conflict that interferes with learning the service motion, you should be able to think through your emotions and master the serve. But don't forget about this conflict; it may pop up again, long after you've mastered the serve. The tensions that interfere with mind-body integration never disappear entirely. If you are in tune with your feelings, you will be ready to confront and reconfront your inner tensions when things get tense on the court. Learning how to do this is the major part of learning tennis.

·4·

Children and Tennis

Tennis used to be a game primarily for adults, but today everyone plays. With the increasing popularity of tennis, teaching programs for all ages have popped up everywhere. Organized tournaments for ages ten to eighteen have become the breeding ground for tomorrow's champions. The media have made culture heroes of Chris Evert Lloyd, Jimmy Connors, Martina Navratilova, Arthur Ashe, and Tracy Austin; seven-year-olds turn off the TV and ask their parents, "Can I play tennis?"; talented adolescent players wonder if they have a professional future on the court.

All this leaves parents with new kinds of decisions to make, decisions for which they are often unprepared. Parents who want to get their kids interested in tennis sometimes don't go about it the right way. And those who never expected their children to take an interest in tennis are often not ready to deal with the potential problems. In this chapter I will be answering the questions asked by parents of children of all ages who are or who will be playing tennis.

When Is a Child
Ready to Learn Tennis?

He could be ready at four or at fourteen. The hidden question behind this one is, "What is motivating your child to want to take up the game?"

The motivation may be a social one; the child may want to play tennis simply because all the other seven-year-olds he knows are learning. Understanding a child's motivation requires talking with the child about what he likes about tennis and why he wants to play, then making tentative steps to encourage him if he seems to have a genuine wish to devote time to it. Don't invest a lot of time and money in tennis unless the child himself spontaneously expresses an interest. If you're dealing with an older child or adolescent, you can be more sure of his motivations. Remember, he doesn't have to become another Rod Laver; there's nothing wrong with wanting to use tennis simply as a mode of social interaction. If your child approaches the game correctly, he will learn to use it as a channel for self-expression. That in itself is valid.

The motivation for a child's wanting to learn tennis may be more than social. If he is introduced to the game by family members, he will usually see it as part of the complex emotional relationships he has with them. Wanting to defeat father or impress mother has been the impetus for many juniors. Such motivations can help or hinder the child's game, depending on how emotionally healthy the family situation is.

But when is the child ready? The answer is, whenever he wants to play badly enough. You as a parent can give him the idea and guide his motivation. But the child will let you know if he's ready or not. As long as he can hold the racquet, he's physically ready; it's up to you to find out whether he is emotionally ready.

> Eight-year-old Andy was eager to play tennis because his older brother played. He had a strong competitive streak in him, and when he asked for lessons, his parents thought it might be a good aggressive outlet for him. But they weren't sure if he was old enough to get anything out of his lessons. They were also worried that he might be too aggressive to go along with the discipline of tennis.
>
> Andy's father spoke with a teaching pro about it, and the pro arranged for him to meet with one of his club's staff members who was particularly good with children. After hearing about Andy, the pro said, "I think you should give it a try. I think I can work with him, show him how to enjoy tennis, and teach him the basics. I've taught a lot of kids his age, and eventually they pick up the game."
>
> When Andy appeared for his first lesson, the pro was ready for his competitiveness. The pro could have predicted that Andy would not be interested in learning the basics, like how to hold the racquet or turn sideways to meet the ball. Andy, im-

patient and excited, just wanted to play points. The pro devised a game in which he awarded Andy one point for hitting the ball, five points for getting it over the net, and ten points if Andy actually won a rally. During Andy's lessons, the pro watched his concentration, and when he saw Andy getting restless he switched from one game to another. Half-hour lessons were about all Andy (and the pro) could take. Andy loved his lessons, and couldn't wait for his next game with his pro.

In this case Andy's desire to play was so strong that his parents felt compelled to arrange lessons for him. They had the good sense to establish a close relationship with a teaching pro who was comfortable working with children of Andy's age and impatience. When the pro suggested additional weekly group lessons to help Andy achieve a more realistic attitude about the game, his parents agreed that Andy was emotionally ready to make the step from tennis as "fun and points" to tennis as a game with rules and real competition. By this time Andy's pro had given him a few tips about the two-handed backhand. Andy handled the group experience with his peers without any real stress.

What clues should a parent look for? If your child seems emotionally mature, is able to tolerate criticism and failure, and can set a goal and work toward it, then he is emotionally ready. Problems arise in those in-between situations in which a child has natural athletic ability but lacks motivation or self-confidence.

Parents may not be able to judge their child's physical and emotional maturity objectively. This is why Andy's father consulted with a tennis pro whose recommendations he trusted. An important part of the decision about the child's emotional readiness is, Ready for what? In Andy's case he was ready for lessons with a sensitive pro who had a good feeling for his competitive aggression. If Andy had started out with group lessons at first, he probably would have been easily frustrated because he needed individual attention and immediate feedback. After a few months of individual instruction he was emotionally ready for the group lessons.

Where Should Your Child Learn to Play? Should You Send Your Child to a Tennis Camp?

The Port Washington Tennis Academy in New York is a good standard to compare with the teaching programs available for your child. The Academy is well known because it promotes a number of national and international junior tournaments and has a well-organized teaching program which was revised in 1971 by Harry Hopman. It provides a facility for young players to attain the goals they set for themselves. Like many top programs, it emphasizes physical fitness, because consistency and endurance usually decide who wins in the ten-, twelve-, and fourteen-year-old junior divisions. The teaching programs are gauged to all levels of playing ability. With beginners, the fun aspect of tennis is emphasized; as the player gains experience the teaching focuses more on strategy and tactics. Training tournaments are arranged to provide an opportunity for players to get "tournament tough" before they compete in sanctioned tournaments.

What about tennis camps? Your child will hear about different tennis camps and read about them in the tennis magazines. Many of these camps have name players like Rod Laver, John Newcombe, Dennis Ralston, and Ken Rosewall associated with them, and for young players especially, seeing a hero at a camp is a special attraction.

I recommend two steps in deciding about tennis camps. The first should be an in-depth evaluation of your child's interest in tennis; the second should be a careful evaluation of the pros and cons of the different tennis camps.

Let's start with your child's interest in attending a summer camp. Find out about his motivation for attending a particular camp. One child may want to go to Newcombe's camp in Florida because it's near Disney World, because it's in Florida, and because something about "Newk" appeals to the child. Whatever camp your child is interested in, make sure his hero is going to be at the camp during the session your child plans to attend.

For many young aspiring tennis players, being taught by Laver or Rosewall can be the thrill of a lifetime. But the child should also have some realistic goals to reach. Most tennis camps recognize the importance of the child having a plan of what he wants to achieve. Ask the camp director what your child can expect to accomplish during the time he attends the camp.

Along with these tennis-oriented considerations, you should also weigh the advantages of a child being exposed to a new environment away from his home. If your child gets edgy on sleep-overs or trips, he may not be ready for an extended stay at a summer camp—tennis or otherwise. But if you feel he will benefit from the experience of meeting children from different parts of the country (and sometimes different countries), then a tennis camp may provide a good learning and culturally enriching experience.

What are the pros and cons of different summer tennis camps? Most of the considerations are practical—but they can make or break your child's experience. Tennis camps are expensive, so first decide whether you can afford to send your child to the camp you feel is suited to his needs. Should he go for a week or a month? Be sure that both you and the child are happy with the length of time he will be away—so that he won't be too lonely away from home, and so that he will have some of the summer left for other activities he enjoys.

Find out about the climate. Some places are better than others if your child has allergies. Does your child do well in heat and humidity, or would he be better off in a cooler climate?

Will your child's friends be attending the camp he plans to attend? Usually it's easier on your child if he knows some of the children who are at the camp, but it's not essential since children make friends quickly. For younger children I recommend going with a friend if possible.

When you examine the camp brochure, check to see if the questions below are answered. If not, write or phone the camp director to find out about your unanswered questions and see if anything has changed since the brochure was printed.

Who does the teaching? What is the ratio of tennis pros to number of children? What is the daily routine? How much tennis will your child get to play? How much of that time will he be supervised? What are the sleeping accommodations like? How many kids are in the same room together? Will your child be in the same room as his friend? What are the ages of the other children? What are the arrangements for feeding the children at the camp? (Most camps provide all the food the child can eat because they realize the importance of nutrition.) What other (nontennis) facilities are available for your child's use? Some camps have interesting activities organized for evening relaxation—tennis movies, lectures, excursions. Lack of these can be the camp's weakest feature; although the child may have had more than enough tennis for one day, he's liable to get bored out of his wits by a steady diet of reading and watching TV every night. If possible, find out how other children have enjoyed the camp. Often that's the best piece of information you can get about a tennis camp.

What Are the Special Problems of Children in Tennis?

The difference between children and adults is development—physical, emotional, and intellectual. These differences in development naturally influence their tennis learning and performance. Parents should be aware of these differences, as they directly bear on the child's involvement in and enjoyment of tennis as a self-mastery sport.

The physical problems of children in tennis are obvious. Kids are smaller than adults. Bigger hands usually wield the racquet with better results. A child or adolescent lacks the strength he will have as an adult, and his coordination is not fully developed. These can constitute problems in playing a good game—but on the other hand, playing tennis helps the child in his physical development. Tracy Austin has proved that with natural athletic ability and good coaching, children can develop fine strokes and compete with adults.

Until the recent popularity of the two-handed backhand, younger children usually had to rely on slice backhands that were immediately spotted as a weakness. Today most children learn the two-hander, emulating Borg, Evert, Austin, and Connors. In many cases their two-handers are stronger than their forehands, so the new strategy against these kids is to play their forehands. With this change in the physical barrier that kept children back a few decades ago, a new era of junior tennis is upon us. Fourteen- and fifteen-year-old girls are winning senior competitions in their home states against women twice their age.

But many younger children are not ready for the physical and emotional stresses of tough competitive tennis. Parents should take special care in assessing their child's physical and emotional strength. Can your child handle the new expectations that come with better teaching methods and improved competition? He may be physically ready to drill hard but may lack the emotional readiness to manage his feelings when a pro is yelling at him with the fervor of a drill sergeant.

> Billy, a nine-year-old with exceptional athletic ability, had taken lessons for two years. He was also a good soccer player because of his strong point—his running ability. His ability to cover the tennis court was remarkable for a child his age.
>
> Billy's pro told his parents that their son had tournament ability, and soon they heard Billy talking about competing in an under-ten state championship. At his pro's suggestion, he took extra lessons and worked out intensively to increase his stamina and get him ready for the tournament.
>
> The day of the tournament came and Billy was in great physical shape. He played well and got into the second round before he was eliminated. Billy took his defeat hard; full of shame, holding back the tears, he tried to act as if it didn't matter. But he wasn't the same for weeks after the match. Though he wouldn't admit it, he had lost his old enthusiasm for tennis. When he forgot to go to his tennis lesson one afternoon, his parents got the message. He had been turned off to tennis.
>
> It wasn't until a few years later that Billy was able to explain to his parents what had happened. For him it had been a disastrous emotional experience, starting with his relationship with the pro. Billy had had grandiose ambitions about tennis, with private fantasies of giving up school and becoming a celebrated tennis prodigy. Neither his parents nor his pro had

seemed receptive to these fantasies, so Billy had kept them to himself and as a result felt emotionally isolated. When the pro started working him relentlessly, Billy felt even more alone and a little misunderstood; he began to hate the drills but was embarrassed to admit it, since he didn't want anyone to think he was a sissy who couldn't take hard work. The running drills were so severe that Billy began secretly to hate running, so that his best ability—which should have been the organizer for his game—became a weakness.

Billy lost the match—and his interest in tennis—because he could not keep his mind and body together under the stress of this emotional conflict. In one sense he wanted to give it up because he had no one who shared his grandiose fantasies and who could help him adapt them to reality.

This is a case where the teaching alliance could have made all the difference. Billy's parents could have been saved the time and money they invested in his tennis, and Billy could have been spared the kind of disappointment that is very hard for a nine-year-old to deal with. His parents could have helped avert disaster by watching his emotional progress in addition to his physical progress. The best measure of how a child is doing with his lessons is how he feels about them. Watch his comments about his teacher; ask him how he feels about his lessons, the games, and the people he plays with; and help him to deal with his fantasies. Many younger children suppress their feelings about the teacher and make a secret of their disappointments, hopes, and frustrations with tennis or with themselves.

In tennis, the line between fun and hard work is a fine one that requires a sensitive appreciation of the child's emotional maturity, physical strength, and motivation. Kenny Rosewall and Rod Laver might have been able to keep up with Billy's pro on the court, but most youngsters of Billy's age aren't ready for such a rigorous training program. Behind the mistake that Billy's pro made was a poor learning alliance; student and teacher weren't communicating well. Billy was not a boy who easily expressed his feelings, and his pro did not pay enough attention to his personality. Unless your child is a constant complainer, keep an ear open for trouble spots in the learning alliance with the idea of helping the pro and your child to work out an effective collaboration.

Another special problem for children learning tennis is their fear of being embarrassed if they can't do what they think their peers or the big kids and adults can do. They may worry that tennis will demand more than they can do. Arthur Ashe suggests decreasing the court dimensions to help younger players feel at home. He also recommends teaching children the net game before they learn ground strokes because so many young children aren't ready for the mature eye-hand coordination tennis demands.

Adolescent girls especially, who have the size, physical strength, and coordination to become fine tennis players, may shy away from the game because they feel awkward, self-conscious about their developing bodies, and hesitant to move freely on the court. Chris Evert Lloyd once said that she was always afraid of being embarrassed by falling on the court. Many girls consider tennis a masculine game and are afraid to let loose on performance. Because of their fear of being embarrassed, they often prefer team sports like volleyball or basketball where the spotlight is not on them alone.

Parents can sometimes encourage their daughters to overcome fear of embarrassment by exerting a little push—as long as it doesn't become pressure. One father told me that he made a deal with his daughter—for every hour she spent with him on the tennis court, he would spend equal time teaching her how to drive a car. Happy to learn to drive, she went along with it. At first she wasn't enthusiastic about tennis, but once she gained self-confidence she began asking her father when they were going to play next. Today she is playing tennis on a college scholarship.

What Are Some Dangers You Should Avoid?

Always guard against being too influential in your child's interest in tennis. Keep in mind that you want tennis to be your child's game so that his learning will be autonomous learning. Don't be afraid to encourage and suggest, but don't push. Also, always remember that your child's interest may be excessively dependent on your emotional support; your discouragement of his interest can hinder or even stop his development as a player. Many young players peak early and then quit because their parents discourage them from taking tennis too seriously.

> Linda, an attractive fifteen-year-old with natural ability, had done well in competitive tennis in the fourteen-and-under grouping. But when she wanted to take extra time to practice for her first sixteen-and-under tournament, her parents cautioned her that she might get poor grades in school as a result of her excessive interest in tennis. They also said that it was about time she started dating, and they weren't happy with her playing tennis so much of the time. Linda worked hard for her next tournament; she had come to value her tennis achievements and was worried that she would not do well against older girls. What would she tell her friends if she didn't get a ranking? What about all the money her parents had put into her lessons and equipment? And if she continued to devote herself to tennis, would she miss out on having a boyfriend? With all these issues at stake, Linda knew she wasn't concentrating in her practice sessions, so she wasn't too surprised when she lost her first round match to a fifteen-year-old.
>
> A few months later, Linda quit tennis altogether. She decided that she wasn't able to handle the stresses of school, social life, and tournament tennis.

Linda's parents had made several mistakes. They made her feel that playing tennis somehow was not a feminine thing to do, and although her grades were good, she began to feel guilty that she wasn't being a serious student. In Linda's mind, playing tennis was interfering with her studies and her social and emotional development. Her parents failed to understand that Linda was faced with the prospect of playing tough matches, against older girls with the benefit of a year's more experience. It was probable they would beat her, and Linda needed help with her feelings about that prospect.

That's why she had wanted to increase the frequency of her practice sessions. If her parents had been more understanding, they might have encouraged Linda to look at her first year in the under-sixteens as an experience year, and not to worry too much about the results. This would have relieved Linda of her burden of responsibility to her family to do well. And her confidence from doing well at tennis would have helped, not hindered, her social life and schoolwork.

Discouraging a child may reflect a deeper problem in the family. Parents who are unconsciously envious of their child's achievements can exert a destructive effect on their child's learning and progress by depreciating their child's achievements or subtly devaluing his ability.

> Dianne, a sixteen-year-old with beautiful strokes, came from a volatile family in which no one minced words about what he thought. Her mother told her point-blank that she lacked the ability to develop further and didn't have the killer instinct she needed to be a winner. "Hang up your racquet," was the obvious message Dianne received.
>
> After this confrontation, the change in Dianne's play was obvious. Her concentration, essential to her fluid strokes, took a holiday. Dianne couldn't contain her rage: "You idiot," she repeatedly muttered to herself, "You just don't have it. Give up!" Dianne had taken on her mother's viewpoint and it obviously interfered with her concentration—destroying her mind-body integration.

Should Your Child Play Competitive Tennis?

So far we have discussed how parents can help their child get started in tennis. The next logical question is, How serious should the child get about tennis? Should he play tournaments? The answer seems obvious: If your child has talent and wants to compete, why not? But it's not as simple as that.

Competitive tennis, in which the child plays publicly for a ranking, puts the child in a completely different world. No matter how competitive his games with friends have been, no matter how much emotional investment he has in tennis, it will be different when he starts playing in tournaments. Although the child may be eager to live out his fantasies of becoming a tennis star, it's up to his parents to assess whether he is able to deal with the stresses of competitive tennis, and to help him understand the motivations behind his ambitions.

A child is emotionally ready for competitive tennis if he is:

—Well motivated to win but not hypersensitive about losing. The child who sulks in his room for an hour after losing a game of Monopoly will not be at ease in competitive tennis, even though he may be eager to try it.

—Socially comfortable with his peers and with adults. The child who cannot relate to others his age, or who is too shy to hold a conversation with adults outside the home, will be unable to cope with the demands of public competition for long.

—Aggressive but not sadistic. A child who is typically resentful, using tennis to lash out emotionally at his opponents, will simply run into more grief on the competitive court. He is better off with a good, psychologically minded teaching pro who can help him to work out his feelings on the court without making lifelong enemies.

—Concerned about his social standing and image but not paranoid about what others think of him. The child who imagines that his schoolmates dislike him or his teachers are out to get him will not be able to function well physically or emotionally in competitive tennis. He may already need professional counseling, and competitive tennis may set him off.

—Able to take disappointments without becoming overwhelmed by frustration. A naturally confident child can feel good about himself even though he feels bad about losing a point. The child who lacks a deep sense

of self-worth may feel hopelessly frustrated by the con
stant challenges of competitive tennis.

A child may, of course, lack some of these qualities and
still be an excellent competitive player. But for such a child,
the competitive arena will not provide optimal enjoyment or
self-expression—and it may leave him with some bitter experiences.

Parents know they should not push a child into something
he doesn't care about. But if your junior has extraordinary
talent, or if you imagine that he might someday blossom, it
may be hard for you to keep from pushing him into tournament play. When you feel this urge, stop and think about
your own motivation. Are you seeing him as an extension of
yourself? Are you trying to live through your child some un-
fulfilled hopes that you had as a child? Try always to bring
the focus back onto your child—*his* capacities, *his* hopes, *his*
feelings about the game. Remember that success in competitive tennis often hinges on the player's autonomy and self-
mastery; help your child make the decision, but *let him make
it.* He should know that you care about him and have hopes
for him, but he should also have the assurance that your feelings about him will be the same whether or not he decides to
play competitively.

Competitive tennis is a serious business these days—especially for American children who have their competitive instincts sharpened from kindergarten on. Children who are
not emotionally prepared for the competition, or who have
been pushed onto the court, can have a hard time of it. For
this reason I recommend caution in making the decision. But
if the child is emotionally equipped to enjoy competitive tennis, if he plays exceptionally well, and if you know that he
wants to do it, then by all means give him a go at it. The competitive tennis experience can be a great boost to maturity,
confidence, and independent functioning. It may not lead to
championship fame, but it will be a positive, healthy mind-
body experience for the child who is suited to it. And it may
even lead to a good professional career.

What Can the Future Provide
for a Top Junior Player?

Tennis has become a glamour sport with big-money prizes. Is there a future for your child in pro tennis? How many talented juniors make it to the top, and what happens to those who don't? We hear the success stories, but we don't hear about the problems and decisions of those who lacked the talent of Borg, Connors, Navratilova, and Tracy Austin. Because only a few make it to the top, Arthur Ashe advises younger players to get a college education first and then, if they like, give the pro circuit a try. Today it's difficult to get on the pro tours without exceptional skill. The competition at qualifying tournaments is fierce. You can be a top player and still find twenty-five other players in your age division who can beat you. Do you quit or keep on trying?

The pro tour is not the only possibility for top juniors. The tennis boom has created a new profession—the tennis teaching pro. Tennis clubs with solid programs for juniors are sought after because parents want their children to be taught by qualified instructors. Tennis camps for kids provide good summer jobs for college students. Many college tennis players moonlight at clubs during the winter months to make extra money. And with more schools offering tennis scholarships to young men and women, there are new opportunities in tennis today.

Because of these opportunities, and in the hope that their children will become top tennis stars, more parents are encouraging their teenagers to invest time and energy in tennis and give competitive tennis a serious try. Tracy Austin practiced five hours a day. Chris Evert Lloyd spent up to eight hours a day working with her father on the ground strokes that have made her famous. Chris feels she got as much out of tennis as she put into it, but she has complained that because of the time and energy she invested in tennis, she missed out on other things. Her comments point to a problem: How can a serious tennis player maintain a balance of interests?

Larry, a fourteen-year-old high-school freshmen and advanced player, had not yet played his first tournament when he asked his father, "Do you think I'm getting too involved in tennis?" Surprised by the question, his father made a joke of it. But Larry persisted and made his father realize that he was very concerned about his future in tennis. Why was he worried? He had hardly got into tennis, and his academic work hadn't suffered for it. Though his father tried to reassure him, Larry told his father that he was afraid of becoming just another sports jock and so he wasn't sure if he wanted to spend four or five days a week at tennis. Larry had a good point. It's hard to be a top player, get good grades, participate in other sports, and have a well-rounded social life.

As difficult as these questions are for younger players, they are more trying for older juniors who realize the importance of top competition if they want a chance to get to the top. High-school graduates facing this dilemma can look for colleges with good tennis and high educational standards, but the competition for these schools is intense. It's difficult to play four or more hours of tennis five days a week and still keep up your studies. Taking easier classes is one solution, but it's not a satisfactory one. Taking a year off at the end of high school or after a few years of college has much to recommend it, since many students feel they get more out of their college years when they are a little older and more mature.

Teenagers need their parents' counsel as much at this time as when they started playing competitive tennis. Tennis is a game of concentration; if the college player is worried about his tennis future, he probably won't think straight on the tennis court. It's a big emotional step for young men and women to say, "I'm going on the tour. I'm going to play tennis full time." This decision requires not only self-confidence, but also firm parental (and often financial) support.

Top juniors have another pressure to contend with when they are not top students or when weekly tournaments keep them away from their books. Regional and national tournaments, which determine national rankings, take the player away from school and usually require both extra tutoring and a tolerant attitude from the school. The financial hardships of traveling to different parts of the country for these tournaments are often defrayed by local and state tennis associations, but these organizations usually cannot finance all the players who want to play these tournaments. Players whose families cannot support a budding Borg's tennis career may have to give up their aspirations unless they live in an area of the country that provides top competition.

Many top juniors don't enjoy traveling from one tournament to the next. Loneliness and depression are frequent complaints, even among the most successful players on the tours.

There are no obvious answers for the hard decisions a talented junior faces. Many find new interests that fit into their intellectual and emotional needs; they decide to hit the books or seek careers and jobs that better fit their needs and aspirations. The uncertainty and pressures of top-flight tournament life stops them from pursuing tennis as a career, and they settle for being proficient at a great game.

Children's tennis has many potential problem spots. But it has many rewards too. Above all, it can be a rich experience in learning and self-expression for the junior player who is guided in the right way.

·5·

Champions

Champions are special. They have become our culture heroes and entertainers. They are complex personalities, at times idiosyncractic, and in spite of being champions, capable of having an off day. But even when Connors loses in straight sets to Jeff Borowiak, or Borg is beaten in his native Stockholm by John McEnroe, they remain our heroes. We know that they will come back strong—or stronger—in the next tournament, because the quality of champions is unshakeable.

What's the difference between the champions and the rest of us? If you practiced as much as Jimmy Connors, could you become a champion? Or if you had the natural talent of Pancho Gonzalez, would *that* make you a champion? Is it good coaching that joins talent and practice to produce the magic formula?

You know by now that none of these factors in isolation produces championship tennis. The special mark of the champs is the self-mastery that shows up in mind-body integration *par excellence.* They all have developed their natural skills into effective competitive weapons, and in doing so they have achieved a supreme confidence that feeds back into their skill and playing style. But each champion is different; each has his own style and his own way of attaining mind-body integration. Let's look at today's most popular stars and see how the "champion factor" works as they deal with the tensions and pressures of topflight competition.

Billie Jean King

Billie Jean King is not only a tennis champion—she has also become a symbol of women's sports. Perhaps no other tennis player has given so much to the game and received so much from it. It's not by chance that her recent book is entitled *Tennis Love* (Macmillan, 1978), for Billie Jean King has been having a love affair with tennis since she discovered the game at the age of eleven. How can we connect this fact with her extraordinary mind-body integration?

One important part of the King story lies in the childhood experiences she has described. Endowed with natural athletic ability and a love for sports, she grew up frustrated by society's restrictive view of the role of women in sports. Like many healthy American girls, she found in athletic activity a gratifying vehicle for self-expression, but at the age of ten she realized that girls weren't "supposed" to be athletes. It was not ladylike. This posed the problem of her life. Her family supported her in sports, and she knew she had talent, but given the situation of women's sports in the fifties, what could she dedicate that talent to? She found the answer in tennis. For Billie Jean King, tennis held the promise of complete self-expression yet did not pose the confrontation with her femininity that soccer or baseball would have. Her complete investment in the game led to her relentless quest for self-definition and personal autonomy. She soon became the champion of the women's cause in professional tennis.

What makes Billie Jean a champion? Watching her play, we admire her strokes, her versatility, and her savvy, but how does she get them together for such a *total* game? The answer hits us as we watch her dramatic court display of every emotion from joy to disgust. And it's no act; she is *feeling* every movement, every stroke; she is *involved* in watching the ball; and she is intensely aware of what she is feeling as well as what her body is doing. The court is her stage for life, and the game *is* her life. More than any other contemporary champion, she achieves total expression of herself in tennis. If choking indicates the presence of suppressed tensions seeking expression, we can see why she's a champion—she experiences and expresses her tensions.

Aggressive tensions are what Billie Jean King is all about when she's on the court. She knows how to face them in herself, and how to experience and express them in harmony

Competitor par
excellence, Billie Jean
King, incredulous over a
line call.

with her physical functioning. Out there with her opponent, the audience, linesmen, and umpires, she doesn't simply engage them—she confronts them. She wants to win, and the intensity of her personal involvement alone is enough to intimidate an opponent. Cross her with a bad call and she'll stare you into stone.

Because tennis is her outlet for complete expression of aggressive tensions, and because she has an almost superhuman will to win, she plays superbly under pressure. "That pressure, the moment of truth when you have to bust your gut, that's what it's all about," she says.[1] Her famous win over Bobby Riggs in 1973 best demonstrates this quality in her. Afterward, Riggs commented that he had underestimated her ability to deal with pressure. The world watched as she assumed the burden of being a symbol for all women players and at the same time coped with Riggs's unnerving antics. She's tough, and pressure just gives her another reason to win.

Because she is so completely involved and able to channel her aggressions into the game, her intellect, emotions, and body are able to feed freely into each other. The result is smooth, powerful functioning. Along with that, her solid intuition tells her when she can elevate her game, put more pressure on the opponent, or rouse the audience to her support. She senses the pace of a match. She *knows* when to do what.

And behind this unique mind-body integration system is hard work. She works as if her life depended on it—and in a sense it does, because tennis is her vehicle for expressing her inner self and for achieving her life's goals.

Bjorn Borg

Unorthodox, innovative, tenacious—these words come to mind in describing the prodigious accomplishment of the Swedish iceman Bjorn Borg. He was the first player to win the Wimbledon Men's Singles four times in a row. Behind his superior mind-body integration is a monolithic emotional in-

"Bjorn has the right kind of courage."—Lennert Bergelin

vestment in tennis. His unparalleled rapid rise to the tennis summit reflects a restless energy that he has channeled into a remarkable commitment to tennis. Beginning at thirteen, when he won his first national junior championship in Sweden, Borg sensed he had a special talent for the game and resolved to become the best. His exaggerated, table-tennis-like topspin forehand suggests his identification with his father, who won a table-tennis championship when Borg was nine years old. With his family's encouragement, Bjorn became a dedicated player. When he won the junior championship, he gave up hockey and soccer to devote all his time to tennis. Behind this decision is part of the answer to the Bjorn Borg mystique—from a very early age he was able to make a total commitment to tennis.

Other champions have had encouragement as juniors, but Bjorn was particularly fortunate to come under the tutelage of Swedish Tennis Federation coach Percy Rosburg, and then former Swedish Davis Cup captain Lennart Bergelin. Seeing the genius behind the boy's unorthodox style, Rosburg did not try to change it—he helped Borg to develop it. Perhaps he realized that Borg's topspin forehand, tactically brilliant as it is, was the key to his supreme self-confidence on the court. Later, Bergelin provided a model for Borg and paved the way for him to focus his energies solely on tennis. Still with Borg, he provides the social maturity, emotional support, and friendship that Bjorn needs to deal with the role of being a champion.

The remarkable thing about Borg's court presence is his consistent tenacity on the court. Borg is like a well-built computer—he won't break down. But this computer has a mind and body of its own. His decisions on the court seem programmed only because of the unfaltering conviction behind them. He feels so sure of his abilities that he never hesitates and rarely chokes. When pressed by an opponent charging the net, ordinary tennis players interrupt the mind-body flow by vacillating about whether they should lob, go down the line, or hit cross-court. But Borg doesn't. He varies his shots, with little concern about choices, because his recovery powers are so great that he feels he'll stay in the point. His style is to challenge his opponent to make one good shot after another. Borg's steadiness, physical strength, and ability to use topspin make him a dangerous opponent. His passing shots are difficult to return because of the dipping motion that comes from the spin. He can hit with pace or spin, or with *both* at once, so you can't win by coming to the net against him, except perhaps on the fastest playing surfaces.

How can you beat him then? Adriano Panatta decided to try to bring Borg to the net, thinking that Borg's Achilles heel might be in his net play. But Panatta lost. No strategy works for long against Borg because he adapts to everything on the court. Even when his volleys lack sting he's so quick at the net that he gets everything back, pressuring his opponent to keep making good shots. Borg usually starts slow, and his opponent may stay with him for a set, but soon Borg begins to collect points, one after another, until his opponent falls apart. No wonder he is described as the stonewall.

Borg's armored-tank approach is an important reflection of his mind-body integration. His ability to move well and run everything down is a physical ability that he has been able to transform into a psychological attitude, a mental toughness. His faith in his method and style is so complete that he doesn't react to winning or losing points—not because he doesn't care about them, but because he *knows* his game is okay. He trusts his skill, his strategy, and his physical and mental reactions.

Borg is also very much in tune with his feelings on the court. He is aware of interpersonal court situations, and he senses whether his mind and body are together or not. When they are, you can't stop him. When they are not, he runs down the cause and does something about it. The impressive factor in his style is his concentration, his single-minded determination. When he feels it slipping, he knows something is wrong either on the court or inside himself. In the 1977 United States Indoor championship, when he felt a linesman had made several bad calls, he refused to continue play until the linesman had been replaced. The bad calls, he said, "were

disturbing my game." In the 1978 Italian Clay Court championship, when the vociferous hometown Italian audience began hurling coins at Borg, he stopped the game and insisted
that the referee control the spectators. Though he's never a
complainer, Borg will assert himself and will not put up with
external interferences with his concentration.

Similarly, he knows when his concentration is being dis-
rupted by his internal state of mind. Who knows why this
happens? For some reason, he occasionally feels "overtennised" and has to make an effort to keep up his concentration. When that happens, he takes a few weeks off, somehow
manages to reorder his inner tensions, and comes back to
tennis eager to play, his concentration intact, his mind and
body one again.

It's no accident that Borg is so sensitive to the internal
harmony behind his concentration. He knows it is the great
strength of his game, and he senses that his big potential
weakness is that feeling of boredom or restlessness that can
destroy his concentration. When he loses his sharpness, it's
because something is pulling him away from his single-mind-
edness. This happened in the early rounds of Wimbledon
1978 and 1979, probably because he was becoming bored by
the lack of challenging opponents.

Borg's game has always been centered on his self-confidence and his ability to concentrate, two intertwined factors
in his development as a player. When he was fifteen, the
Swedish Davis Cup committee named him to play in the fi-
nals. He reacted to this honor much as Tilden had—it helped
him to believe in his possibilities and set him to work on his
mind-body integration. He pinpointed concentration as the
factor he needed to work on. Just as Tilden had drilled with
his backhand, Borg practiced concentration. He went at his
practice sessions as if they were matches, and set himself the
goal of maintaining concentration for two hours at a time.
This led him to a decisive breakthrough that still shows in
his intense playing style. He says that, even now, his "secret"
is reminding himself to concentrate before matches. Concentrating on concentration is the key to his game. Once he is

fully concentrated, he can function freely in the knowledge that he can win.

Part of Borg's functioning is using his head as well as his emotions and physical skill. Lennart Bergelin has helped him to do this, and Borg has come up with many a surprise for his opponents. In the 1976 Wimbledon tournament, just when the opposition was trying to figure out how to get him off the baseline, he switched tactics and started playing the net, throwing his opponents off balance. In the 1977 Pepsi-Cola Grand Prix, he combined lobs and chip shots to outsteady Jimmy Connors. In 1978, still improving in confidence and strategic ability, he won the Pepsi-Cola Grand Prix by increasing his depth and flattening out his strokes, playing his own game as hard as he could.

Like all champions, he keeps improving. One commentator, noticing Borg's game getting better and better, wondered, "What will happen when the kid gets a good forehand volley?" After his fourth straight Wimbledon victory, one wonders how far he can go. His unique ability to hit out with full determination has made him one of tennis's great champions. And he's still growing!

Jimmy Connors

No player can rival Jimmy Connors in engaging, provoking, and amazing the tennis world. For sheer entertainment value, he's top dollar. His individuality, tenacity, raw power, self-confidence, and unpredictability keep us watching to see what he'll do next. But more than anything, the key to his game is aggression; he doesn't *play* an opponent—he *attacks*. Defiant, rebellious, feisty, he steels himself for each point, with one intention: to murder the ball. Few people could handle the enormous aggression Connors has inside him, but he has managed to channel it into a winner's style.

Pressure is his forte. He creates it and maintains it. Never one to suppress his feelings, he has developed a court style that gives his aggression full vent. His style and court antics go together. Connors, more than any player in modern tennis, pushes his aggressions to the limit, using anything and everything he can to mobilize himself. Chris Evert Lloyd says, "The madder he gets, the better he plays. Jimmy can't beat someone he likes. He has to hate the player he's playing." He antagonizes not only his opponent but also the audience. "I like to have fans against me," he says. "I want to do everything I can to get them against me more. When they're yelling at me, I really get into the match."[2] He combines this tremendous hostility with an intense concentration on goals. He may joke with a spectator before gearing himself for the next point, but his mind is so focused on the match that he won't remember what he said. Whether he is clowning, making obscene gestures, or exploding into a tantrum, Jimbo is always thinking of the next ball and how to smack it.

It's clear that his mother has been a determining force in his becoming a champion. She set him to playing with tennis balls and a racquet when he was a year old. As he developed and started learning, she taught him to use the two-hander because it was the only way he could control the racquet. Pushing him on and guiding his every learning step, perhaps she made him feel that he had to keep doing better, had to put his whole self into the game without ever letting up. "It's like a marathon," Connors has said. "You have to find that final kick. You grab a little guts, grab a little anything you have down there and pull it up when you need it."[3] From that early beginning, Connors developed his famous two-handed backhand, which Dick Stockton considers is Connors's greatest weapon. Stockton says, "Jimmy's backhand is extra tough to play against because he attacks the ball so well. He likes to take the ball early, taking it on the rise. The timing has to be perfect in order to take the ball on the rise consistently and successfully."[4] Connors learned to do this when he played in an armory in St. Louis, where the ball skidded on wooden boards. If you didn't play it early, it went right by. The natural player to coach him in this was Pancho Segura, who had developed a two-handed forehand to increase his ground-stroke power. So when he was sixteen, Connors's mother sent him to Segura, who recognized immediately that

"No matter how much they hate me, they have to respect the way I play."

Connors was champion material. He encouraged Connors to take the ball on the rise rather than give the opponent time to prepare while the ball comes down. Connors learned the method and later made it popular. Segura also helped him to integrate his mental toughness and concentration with his natural skills.

Connors's biggest physical strength is probably his extraordinary eye-hand coordination. He seems to see the ball earlier, so it's easier for him to take it on the rise. His capacity for innovation is also remarkable. What he does is combine these skills into an attack built around his ground strokes. The result is a hard game. Some players and fans don't like it—they feel that Connors has changed tennis from the shot-maker era of Laver to a bullish pressure game. "Where is sportsmanship?" they ask. "Where are the aesthetics and finesse of a Rosewall backhand or an Orantes lob?" But Connors's fans respond by saying, "Never mind. Here are the results."

Serving has always posed a problem for him. He has been criticized for his unorthodox toss. But when he has mind and body together—which is most of the time—he can penetrate with his serve effectively enough to allow his aggressive ground strokes to take over. Connors doesn't try to win outright with his serve. As with all his strokes, he aims for the lines. But if he is serving badly, he concentrates on getting good depth with his first serve to reestablish his mind-body integration.

Because of his aggressive style of play and his unpredictable behavior, what we notice first about Connors is not his game but his image. This is fitting, because his image is an important form of his self-expression. He boosts his self-esteem by getting top results on the tennis court. But he expresses his inner aggressive tensions by behaving the way he does. He loves to stand up to authority, to fight injustice and assert his convictions. He hits out and speaks out. A creature of the present, he hates to be tied down to anything. He'll do a little dance when he gets the point, and he'll make an obscene gesture when things go wrong. He is motivated partly by hatred and partly by an ideal instilled in him by his mother and fostered by his coach Segura. As a player he is still growing. Since 1975, when he reached the top and decided to let himself go, both physically and mentally, he has shown signs of consolidating his court style and behavior into a new maturity. After about six months of weight gain and an active social life, he thought things over, called on the support of his mother, and returned to the old discipline. But he has been subtly different ever since, and has gained in respect and popularity because of it.

Connors likes it at the top, partly because it brings out in him resources he wasn't sure he had. When Borg trounced him in Wimbledon 1978, Connors was visibly stung. The defeat was bad enough, but in addition his press and fans seemed to be questioning whether the basic Connors style was sound. This was the challenge he needed to arouse his aggression, and he went on to recapture his United States Open crown at the 1978 Flushing Meadows final.

At the root of Connors's mind-body integration is something he himself never forgets: his learning experience with his mother. He acknowledges that his style originates from practice sessions with her. She taught him from the beginning that lines were there to be hit. That ideal has never changed for him. Living up to it keeps him sharp and alert, always improving, always on top of the battle.

Chris Evert Lloyd

Chris Evert Lloyd is a very different kind of champion. The crowds don't love her, the crowds don't hate her. Sometimes they're even bored with her because she doesn't bring to the court that dramatic tension that spices a good championship match. When you go to an Evert Lloyd match, you see good sound tennis playing. What else did you want?

She is mature for her age. She is not about to let go with hostile emotional exhibitions or crowd-pleasing antics. She'll tell you about her feelings, but won't care much what you think about them. She survived being the teen queen of tennis, and maintained her personal dignity throughout her publicized romance and breakup with Jimmy Connors.

Caring about winning seems to be an important factor in Chris Evert Lloyd's mind-body integration. She comes from a strong tennis family—her father, two sisters, and a brother are fine players—and she played tennis from her grade-school years on. But she didn't really care about her game until she was an adolescent. She says, "It happened when I started to win. That's when things started to change inside. When I was six or ten, I could lose matches at love and love and I didn't care at all."[5] But at the age of twelve or thirteen her motives began to solidify and she started playing to win.

Since Chris hit the top so young, she has had to contend with more pressures than most champions. One of the important pressures was making the normal adolescent move toward autonomy (the break from her parents) while at the same time coping with her new identity as international champion. Her parents had always been supportive, strict, and encouraging. From her father she had learned high standards of stroke production; her mother had always been there to protect and help Chris, and accompanied her on all her tours. At eighteen, with the United States Clay Court championships and Wimbledon ahead of her, Chris found herself wondering about her ambitions in tennis and how she should pursue them. She describes that year as being an unhappy one; she felt the need for emotional independence and sensed the relationship between her emotional growth and her prowess on the tennis court. The inner tensions grew and took their toll—she fell into a slump, losing all the big matches that summer. But she realized what was behind it. "It really was an emotional slump," she says.[6]

The major factor in pulling out of this slump was her decision to win *for herself* and *by herself.* She decided to go it alone and asked her mother to leave the tour. She doesn't talk much about what happened during this period of her life, but she must have come to a better understanding about the correlation between her life on the court and her inner emotional life. Now married to British Davis Cupper John Lloyd, Chris continues to achieve success on the court.

"It's not in my nature to keep losing, and coping with it. I couldn't live with losing."

"I want to win. I like it. I need it," Chris says.[7] Being a champion turns her on, keeps her going. The threat of losing her dominance, of being second best, has always been the greatest stimulus for her to work harder. Because she is so consistently good, she has no underdog appeal; the crowd is always eager to see the queen toppled from her throne, so it's business as usual for Chris to find herself facing a hostile crowd and a fired-up opponent. But this is when she is toughest. She has superior concentration and nerves under pressure, and she won't give in. You can never count her out until the match is over.

Although she lacks the grace of Evonne Goolagong and the powerful physique of Martina Navratilova, Chris has two important qualities going for her: concentration and confidence. She plays percentage tennis. She is accused of being an unexciting player because she is so consistent that she usually just wears her opponents down. She makes few spectacular shots—her ground strokes are solid, strong, and deep. She creates intense pressure on her opponent just by playing so unvaryingly well for so long, her whole self concentrated on her game, her whole self believing in the superiority of her game.

Behind Chris Evert Lloyd's mind-body integration is her extraordinary orientation to winning. For her, this doesn't mean worrying about points and results; it means dedicating herself to the more abstract goal of being number one, and doing what is necessary—including intensive practice—to achieve and maintain the goal. Nothing makes her work harder than a threat to her dominance. In tiebreakers or in a long third set, she invariably comes up with her best shots, as she demonstrated in her 1979 pre-Wimbledon win (7-5, 5-7, 13-11) over Navratilova. Every few years one of her arch rivals seems to get the edge for a while, and that's all that Evert Lloyd needs to push herself into shape. When Evonne Goolagong was on her game in 1976, Chris was unbeatable. And in early 1978 Navratilova's powerful serve and volley game was getting Chris down, but it soon turned into an impetus for her to improve. In a matter of months, she won the

United States Nationals at Flushing Meadows and then, opt-ing for a full rerun to circuit play, again demonstrated her dominance in women's tennis by defeating Navratilova twice—in Atlanta and in a European indoor championship match.

Chris Evert Lloyd needs to excel. She doesn't worry about her weaknesses, she just works to improve them. Of course she isn't invulnerable to criticism, and she is probably most sensitive about the fact that she is not considered to be the "complete" tennis player. Her play at the net is not the best, and she is still not fully confident about it. She is so superior at the baseline that she doesn't need to win at the net, but she does feel the need to improve her net play and become more versatile. Similarly, her serve has given her problems, and she has done much to improve it in the last few years. Because she has it together psychologically, she does not let her weaknesses affect her mind-body integration. And as Bud Collins once commented, "If she gets her volleys down, they can close the tournaments."

Tracy Austin

"She's a coming champion, that's for sure," said Bobby Riggs in 1976, when Tracy was thirteen. "She'll either be the best in the world by sixteen or seventeen, or she'll never be. She'll peak very early."[8] One year later, Tracy Austin, a vision of pigtails, braces, and poise, won her first round at Wimbledon, proving herself a champion contender and heralding the next great rivalry anticipated in tennis: Austin vs. Evert Lloyd. She turned pro at fifteen and won her first major tour tournament in West Germany by reversing a previous defeat by Betty Stove. At this writing she is the youngest woman to have won the U.S. Open championship. No doubt she's a champion, but can she live up to her promise and become the world's premier player?

Tracy has the advantages of being bright, physically gifted, talented, and well coached. She is good not only at tennis but also at soccer and baseball, and she's a straight-A student.

Her family lives and breathes tennis; her three brothers are top players and her sister is a teaching pro. Tracy may grow tall—her sister is close to six feet and one brother is six-four. Not only has Tracy been playing tennis since she was old enough to see the ball coming, but she has also had good coaching. Her mother, a fine player herself, saw to that.

Tracy's coach, Robert Lansdorp, was at first cautious about her prospects, because he had seen too many top juniors peak prematurely and fizzle out. And her size made him wonder too. "When I first saw Tracy," he says, "I wasn't that gung ho. She was so *little.* I could see potential, but I wouldn't have said, 'Oh, Mrs. Austin, she's going to be the greatest.' It is a long process to become a champion, but gradually I saw greatness in her."[9]

What's special about Tracy? She wins. Her mind-body integration is easier, smoother, faster, more advanced. When she works hard, she learns. Part of the way she does this is by using her mind. She thinks about her game intellectually. As Lansdorp says, "She learns quickly and accepts criticism. She can tell you what she did wrong without asking."[10] According to him, if he doesn't push her, she becomes disappointed. This is an unusual trait in one so young, but Tracy Austin is an unusual player. Her parents helped her along the way, always being supportive, setting up ideals but never forcing them on Tracy. Her mother says, "I never set goals for [my children]; they set their own goals so it was always fun."[11]

Well, almost always fun. It turns out that Tracy doesn't like to lose any more than her rival, Chris Evert Lloyd. At nine, Tracy announced to her mother that she wanted to be the number-one player in the world. She has her goals set, and she works hard to achieve them. But she has yet to suffer the disappointments along the way. As a child champion playing against women twice her age, nobody really expected her to win, so it was almost a lark for her to trounce Sue Barker or Bobby Riggs. It was a little different when she played against girls her own age. As she put it, "The pressure is more intense, because I'm supposed to win."[12] But her

"I don't tense up when I play anybody."

game seems to be unaffected by pressure; mind-body integration unclouded, she gives the match her all regardless of external pressures—and she usually wins.

The tennis world waits for her to grow up and wonders how physical and psychological maturity will change her game. What shifts in mind-body integration will come about as her interests, her emotions, and her body change? She is so cool and able under pressure now that some think her bubble has to burst sooner or later. "I wonder if she knows what's going on yet," said Billie Jean King when Tracy impressed the fans at Forest Hills in 1977. "That's great. She's winning. Wait'll she learns how to choke."[13] And Vic Braden has commented, "As she gets older ... the question will be whether she can handle the pressure and have sound strokes in all departments."

It's difficult to assess child or adolescent champions because they lack experience and are not fully developed physically or emotionally. Mind-body integration depends on the harmonious interplay between mind and body; growing into adult mind-body patterns causes shifts in this interplay and can greatly affect tennis performance, just as it affects all other areas of life. But what we see in Tracy Austin shows promise of continued championship. Her repeated wins over Navratilova and Evert Lloyd marked her as a contender for the tennis summit. She has what it takes to stay on top; motivation because of a supportive family and coach to guide and encourage her; physical ability backed up by hard work; and a gift for learning, concentrating, and seeing herself objectively. Her one weakness: her serve, which is bound to improve with the years. Her biggest strength: a need to win, along with the confidence that she can satisfy that need.

Martina Navratilova

Navratilova is not everybody's idea of a champion. At sixteen she became a serious international contender; at eighteen she had become known for her powerful serve and net play; at nineteen her game fell apart; and at twenty-two, she came

"Someone will have to beat me. I will not beat myself."

back strong and steady. Without doubt she can be number one. The big question is whether she will do so.

With powerful wrists and forearms, height to play the big game, and the strongest serve in women's tennis, she has the physical attributes of a champion. Her ease of movement is extraordinary in a woman of her size; she moves fast and confidently. The baffling ups and downs of her career reflect her mercurial disposition and point up the important role of emotions in mind-body integration.

In looking at the evolution of her game so far, her 1976 collapse stands out for its developmental significance. She had gained celebrity status, money, and freedom. Three years after her defection from Czechoslovakia, she had made it to the top on her own. Suddenly she toppled. Françoise Durr trounced her 6-1, 6-1 on the Virginia Slims circuit, and Janet Newberry edged her out in three sets at Forest Hills. She gained twenty pounds, lost her timing, developed tendinitis, and choked constantly. As she well knew, the physical problems behind her performance breakdown were the result of a profound emotional low. She was depressed, underconfident, undisciplined, and emotionally out of control on the court. She dealt with pressure by playing poorly and screaming at court officials. Later, she said, "The whole thing was becoming too much. Everybody told me how great I was and how I should win easily and be number one, and I knew it really wasn't that easy. I had difficulty coping with the whole situation—other people's expectations, the defection, missing my family."[15] Perhaps it was only a normal reaction for a naturally volatile woman who had soared to success so young, while at the same time making the transition from adolescent to adult and dealing with the emotional trauma of losing a family and homeland. Having to handle all this, along with the high-pitched pressure to stay on top, is enough to overwhelm any healthy nineteen-year-old.

The remarkable part of it is what has happened since 1976. Navratilova is back and better than ever. Determined, confident, and in top physical shape, she has whipped King, Evert Lloyd, Austin, and Goolagong, and plans to keep the pressure up. Her concentration rarely falters, and though she still has a sharp tongue for disputing a line call, her complaints are less frequent and now resemble healthy self-expression more than temper tantrums. All in all, she has reintegrated her mind and body.

How has she done it? Her first step had to be facing up to her emotional crisis in terms of what it meant to her life and her tennis performance. This is a private experience which only Navratilova can evaluate, but she has hinted at its significance by saying, "I've learned to listen to myself, rather than to everyone else. No one else has gone through my experiences, and no one knows me better than myself."[16] Once she had confronted her emotional tensions, she was able to see more clearly what she wanted and how she could achieve it. She gradually realized that she needed three things to set her straight: supportive guidance, recuperation, and discipline. Supportive guidance was probably the most important of the three. This she found in her friend Sandra Haynie, former pro golfer, whom Navratilova hired as manager and adviser and who became her constant companion. Haynie's first move was to turn the pressure off, and she got Navratilova to take an entire month away from tennis and dedicate it to total relaxation. That was that. Mentally stronger, the champ then started to work, following a regimen of two ninety-minute workouts daily on the court, along with an hour a day on a Nautilus machine to build up strength. The emotional support and guidance, along with a balanced disciplinary program, put Martina back on her feet. Little by little, she came back. Within a year she had triumphed at Wimbledon and at several Virginia Slims tournaments. She knows what happened and how important a supportive relationship can be in helping to restore mind-body integration. Speaking of Haynie, she says, "How she helps me is more psychological than technical. She has had a calming effect on me. She understands pressure."[17] Simply having someone who can understand your weaknesses as well as your strengths, and who can see you objectively at the same time, is sometimes the magic formula needed.

Navratilova is a proven champion. But at this writing it's anyone's guess whether her performance has stabilized permanently or not. Has she latched onto a solid style of coping with external pressures and internal tensions, or will she fall into a pattern of emotional fluctuations that leave no room for the full development of her enormous winning potential? Her dramatic 1976 slump left some wondering if she could cope with the pressures of being on top. But she has shown that she can get her act together, and as her Wimbledon triumphs show, she is learning to keep it together. She's a champion worth watching.

Guillermo Vilas

This powerful Argentine, who writes poems about loneliness and death, brought a different kind of image to the champions' court. He came to the game with natural talent and a lot of strength; he liked tennis for its many options and possibilities for self-expression. In every point he found a challenge.

Vilas played in the early seventies during and after his short-lived career as a law student, but for him tennis was only one of many interests into which he channeled his creativity. His ground strokes were consistent, he was a good retriever, and he hit with pace—but something was lacking. He was not a consistent winner; his serve was weak, his volley substandard. He often showed a lack of confidence, and his inner tensions often robbed him of the ability to concentrate and left him feeling hurt and angry on the court.

Then in 1975 Vilas turned to his friend, Ion Tiriac, a former Rumanian Davis Cup player. Tiriac became not only his coach but the integrating force in a new mind-body integration that has brought Vilas to the level of champions.

Tiriac took over and reworked Vilas both physically and mentally. He devised practice sessions for Vilas that would have made Vince Lombardi wince. Service motion drills increased Vilas's control and power; tough volley drills prepared him for the ultimate confrontations with Borg and Connors. Tiriac somehow knew how to bring out and focus

"I think I never have the killer instinct, but sometimes you have to be very strong in the head."

Vilas's aggression; he taught Vilas how to attack and create pressure on his opponents. He provided emotional strength and strategic advice that gave Vilas the confidence he had lacked. With Tiriac behind him, Vilas's game came together. He has stayed with Tiriac and claims that his game depends on Tiriac's coaching: "If Tiriac should leave me, I would be lost. I lean on him. I put myself completely in his hands and do whatever he tells me."[18]

It is a strange teacher-student relationship, not the usual one recommended for champions. How has it led to the extraordinary improvement in Vilas's mind-body integration? Vilas has to be understood not only as an artist in tennis but also as a person who needs others to help him realize his potential. Many creative individuals with unrealized or unexpressed talent achieve success only when they are supported by a close relationship with a mentor/authority figure who dominates and structures the artist's work and emotional life. When it comes to playing championship tennis, Vilas is this kind of person. He functions on his own when writing a poem or screenplay. But in the channeling of his aggressions on the court, he needs an alter ego. He needs Tiriac to win— the two of them together produce one superb mind-body integration, with Tiriac counseling and pushing, Vilas slugging and performing.

Since Tiriac remade him, Vilas has been able to channel his natural power into dominance. Discipline has been a large part of it. But the most remarkable improvement is in his ability to concentrate fully, in practice and on the court. This shows up mainly in his new consistency with ground strokes. "Now I concentrate 100 percent," he says.[19] For Vilas, facing his inner tensions and sharpening his concentration has been the key to mind-body integration.

Evonne Goolagong

At nineteen, Evonne Goolagong won the center-court final at Wimbledon 1971, defeating Margaret Court 6-4, 6-1. Her unparalleled movement on the court, her accurate passing

A picture of natural athletic coordination, poise, and grace.

shots, and her unique capacity to elevate her game were qualities that marked her as one of tennis's most gifted champions.

Goolagong is what we call "a natural"—an intuitive player whose instinct for the game is her greatest asset. But she knows how to use intellect along with instinct; capable of shrewd tactical play, she can break up an opponent's rhythm spontaneously by unpredictable slices and spins.

She is graceful and feminine, and at the same time she comes off as an aggressive winner. This is part of her style—a style that is distinctively hers and has not undergone significant change during the last decade. When she is playing well she can win point after point, but once in a while she loses concentration and "falls asleep" on the court, in a lapse that Australian player Kim Warwick calls a "walkabout." Strangely enough, her losses often occur after her winning streaks; it's as if she has used up all her confidence. Suddenly she falls into unforced errors and fizzles out. But these lapses occur infrequently enough and are balanced by her unique physical abilities when she is on her game.

Critics say that Evonne should pressure her opponents by going to the net more often, but that's not the way she works. She plays each point intuitively, sensing the right moves and following her inclinations. When this brings her to the net, she sometimes wins the point. But when she is hot, Evonne wins no matter where she is on the court. If her second serve fails her and her opponent tries to capitalize by taking the net, Evonne demonstrates the most accurate passing shots in women's tennis. And she can outrun her toughest rivals.

Her survival instinct makes her one of the great retrievers of tennis. When she is fully concentrated on her game, she is so intense that she creates her own special brand of pressure. Most players react to her physical superiority by pressing too much; when this happens, Goolagong usually lets go with her superior footwork and natural coordination, impervious to the pressure of her opponents.

Following the birth of her daughter a few years ago, Goolagong made a successful comeback. She has felt a conflict of interests in being a mother and a tennis champ, but she has managed to do both. Because of her financial success in women's professional tennis, she is able to play the tour, traveling with her husband, baby, and nurse. The difficult part was getting back into shape after her pregnancy. She had never had to condition herself before, but she lifted weights, jumped rope, and jogged herself back to stardom. The support of her husband, Roger Cawley—a good player in his own right—helped her over this difficult time in her career. In 1977 and 1978, Evonne was plagued by a series of foot injuries, but by the spring of 1979 had again returned to form. The fall she defeated Tracy Austin and won the U.S. Women's Indoor Singles championship.

What's the big factor in Goolagong's mind-body integration? It's a natural ability to be herself and express herself, without major tension hang-ups. Perhaps the support of others—from coach Vic Edwards when she was a child, and from her husband in later life—has been an important part of her physical and emotional togetherness. Always the fluent tennis player, she seems to improve just a little over the years. She's a born champion.

Ilie Nastase

Imagine the following scenario. Wimbledon, the ultimate in tennis tradition. You are down two sets to one and your opponent has won that all-important seventh game to break serve and take a 4-3 lead. He's a consistent player. He doesn't choke. He beat you on grass at Forest Hills a few years ago. What's your strategy?

    A. Play cheerleader with the crowd.

    B. Clown with the linesman.

    C. Hide behind a screen at the far end of the court (out of sight, out of mind).

    D. All of the above.

If you're Ilie Nastase and the year is 1977, you'll choose **D** and defeat Andrew Pattison 7-9, 3-6, 7-5, 8-6, 6-3.

Ilie defies definition. Perfectionist; master shot maker; court clown; intuitive tennis artist; brilliant, charming, arrogant, powerful. He is the most controversial and poorly understood player in contemporary tennis. Connors's antics draw some boos, but Nastase's behavior disrupts play. What kind of champion is this?

Nastase is exciting, but he is also irritating. His selfish disregard for the conventions of fair play can be offensive. He doesn't cheat, but when he stalls, he breaches court etiquette and interrupts his opponent's rhythm; and when he stops to berate a linesman, his opponent must wait until Nasty's performance is over. Penalty points and fines do nothing to change his behavior. But Arthur Ashe, as mistreated by Nastase on the court as anyone, has pointed out that Ilie is a perfect, gracious gentleman when he is off the court. And Don Fontana, who went after Ilie's neck after the champ stopped trying in a Canadian Open final, has conceded that it's hard to dislike Nasty. For a while his outraged critics wanted Nastase out of the game, but later a second reaction of acceptance and sympathy developed for him. The tennis world senses Nastase's personal struggle on the court, and has come to a larger view of him.

In the past few years, Nastase has shuffled from World Team Tennis matches and exhibitions to Grand Prix and World Championship Tennis tournaments, and the heavy load is beginning to show. One day the old magic is there; the next he's lost his touch and overpresses or outfinesses himself against top players like Borg, McEnroe, and Vilas.

What happens when he steps on the court? When he's himself, he's a player of superior ability—that's why he holds the edge on Jimmy Connors over the years. But Nastase has a problem with his concentration. As high-strung as a truckload of Borg racquets, he flares at the slightest distraction. But he's aware of what's going on. "I never get angry without reason, but sometimes the tiniest, simplest thing will set me off. Everyone thinks I have it in for my opponent, but it is really myself that I am mad at. With someone else, he might flub an important shot and take it badly. But with my

"... a perfect, gracious gentleman—when he's off the court."—Arthur Ashe

nature, I take it three times as badly. I get carried away. I can't control myself."[20]

The Nastase ethic is to win—by any means. When he sees that his game is not a winning one, he fragments. One gets the idea that losing is like death on the court to him. If the tournament conditions (the court, the officiating, the crowd's behavior) interfere with his mind-body integration, he rages. Winning is so important to him that in the heat of a match he always feels some justification for his behavior, but afterward he realizes just how much he's been carried away by his emotions.

When Nastase has it together, he can maintain the highest levels of mind-body integration. His natural gifts for the game, competitive spirit, and artistic flare come together to produce extraordinary tennis. But when he fragments, he rages first inside, and then—if he's distracted by external or internal conditions—at his opponent, the audience, the umpire, or the linesman. When he loses his equilibrium, no holds are barred. Trapped by his mood and unable to reverse his behavior, his game falls apart.

Fortunately, he's not consistent in this style. Much of the time he is able to overcome his limitations and play effectively. This is because he is aware of his problems, openly acknowledges them, and realizes that his inability to manage his feelings better has lost him a number of important matches. At least four integrating factors determine the quality of his play: successful execution on the court, winning play, demonstrating his mastery, and pleasing his audience. The common theme is positive feedback; without it, his concentration becomes strained and his confidence weakens. Usually his concentration goes first, and his antics can be seen as a desperate effort to bolster his confidence. His restless agitation also reflects his inability to sustain the intensity of the feelings he experiences on the court. As he says:

> The truth is, it's impossible for me to maintain maximum concentration for several hours without a moment's relaxation. So

I modify my approach, but believe me, it's not easy for me either. I clown around? Right. My opponent might lose his concentration? Right again. But what about me! I'm the one who gets the most bothered, the most distracted.[21]

Somehow his capacity to catch up with his feelings enough of the time keeps him on top.

John McEnroe

John McEnroe is riding a tiger of talent, driving perfectionism, and emotional intensity that may take him to the top of men's professional tennis. At nineteen, John's superior skills became apparent when he put together a string of four titles in eight singles tournaments, including a 6-3, 6-4 victory over Bjorn Borg in the 1978 Stockholm Open. In this match John served and volleyed brilliantly, leaving Bjorn perplexed on the fast indoor surface. A few months later, John again demonstrated his extraordinary racquet control and stroke mastery by winning the 1979 Masters championship in New York. He defeated Jimmy Connors in a preliminary round and then came from behind to edge Arthur Ashe in the final. With his wins over Borg and Connors, and his record-breaking performance in leading the United States to a 4-1 victory over Great Britain in the 1978 Davis Cup final, McEnroe became the sensation of the tennis world. Add six doubles championships in the last half of the 1978 tennis season and his 1979 U.S. Open victory and it's no wonder that the tennis world began asking, "What lies behind John McEnroe's meteoric rise to tennis stardom?"

A large part of the answer lies in John's emotional intensity and his perfectionistic need to play his best. His talent and emotional intensity go hand in hand. Because of them, he can't disguise his self-disgust whenever he makes a mistake. Like many high-strung virtuoso talents, John becomes infuriated when he fails to perform to his own personal standard. His faces, foot-stomping, and obscene gestures create an image of *l'enfant terrible*. But when he's on the court, he's so

"Against Connors and Borg you feel like you're being hit with a sledgehammer. But this guy is a stiletto.... He's got a ton of shots."—Arthur Ashe

immersed in the match that he scarcely realizes the intimidating effects of his glaring at opponents and linesmen. His volatile temper and obscene gestures are invariably compared to the antics of Ilie Nastase and Jimmy Connors, but Nastase argues that in this department it's no contest—McEnroe is worse than he and Jimmy combined! Although some sportswriters have urged tennis fans to "forget about McEnroe's transgressions and concentrate on his ability,"[22] his reputation for dark Irish moods and emotional outbursts persists.

John's temperamental behavior and driving perfectionism are parts of a whole cloth. His ability to link his emotionality to his physical play allows him to take risks that other leading players steadfastly avoid. But to play the way John does requires total emotional investment, and when things go wrong, he is left with pent-up emotion that sometimes leads to bouts of choking.

When he was twelve and began taking tennis seriously at the Port Washington Tennis Academy, John immediately caught Harry Hopman's attention. Hopman was impressed with his talent, especially his racquet work. Because of John's left-handed serve and his ability to chip and stroke with spin, Hopman envisioned another Neale Fraser. John was a quick learner and learned a great deal under Hopman's supervision, but they never established the emotional rapport needed to maintain a learning alliance. Between John's problems with authority figures and Hopman's intolerance of the boy's court antics, the two had a falling out. Hopman respected the boy's talent, but he couldn't deal with John's anger and immaturity.

It wasn't until John joined forces with his next coach, former Mexican Davis Cup competitor Tony Palafox, that John achieved the mind-body integration that has led to his extraordinary climb in the men's tennis rankings. He began to grow up. McEnroe and Palafox established a good learning alliance based on mutual respect. Palafox recognized John's potential and was especially impressed with John's ability to learn quickly and to use what he learned on the court. Out of his need to confront authority figures, John tested his mentor repeatedly, but Palafox was patient and weathered the stormy periods. He rounded out John's tennis education by helping him to develop an all-court game. He helped John improve his abilities to change pace, play angles, and serve and volley. John's speed and versatility, and especially his gift for touch, allowed Palafox to help him develop his outstanding stroke repertoire. But Palafox's most important contribution was probably his work with John to improve the timing and coordination of his serve. About his improved serve John says, "I lean in now on my first serve, and maybe it looks a little weird, but it helps me to get my rhythm going and also helps me to hit the ball out in front, with my body fully extended. In that way, I can get a lot more power on my serve and still keep it in."[23]

What does the future hold for tennis's new superstar? When asked about his aims and goals, John usually answers that he wants to get better and better. When he is happy with his game, he feels he can beat anyone in the world. He attributes his increasing self-confidence to his work with Palafox and to his Davis Cup and tournament success. When talking about reaching the top of the tennis world, John shows his rapidly developing maturity. He wants to be number one, but he's not obsessed with it. "I think as long as I'm progressing and playing well, that's the important thing. I'm not worried about having to be number one by the next year or two. I mean, I'll try to reach number one. I hope I have a chance to. But if I don't . . . as long as I'm happy playing, that's all right."[24]

What Makes a Champion?

Mind-body integration is the key to championship play. The champions are endowed with natural physical skill, but they also have different combinations of talent, drive, determination, and psychological needs that push them to the top. Champions know how to learn and develop. Jimmy Connors comments that many of the top players have good physical ability, but it's *how they use what they have* that makes the difference.

Champions come in all sizes, as Kenny Rosewall proved with magnificent ground strokes that compensated for his lack of height and power. And each of them has his own characteristic playing style—a style that can't be copied. As Bergelin has pointed out, during the mid-forties everyone tried to imitate Jack Kramer's big game, not realizing that other styles would one day be a part of championship tennis.

It's tempting to say that the integrating factor for the champions is ego—the personality strength that makes them confident and able to work harder on their game. But when we look into the background of these players and think about the interplay between their personal ambitions, temperament, and style, we discover that each champion has a unique integrating factor. We also have to consider that they all were helped along by family background, good coaching, and the opportunity to play and practice.

These essentials help champions to deal with the elements that all players must contend with—managing feelings on the court, coping with line calls, keeping equilibrium when the audience is booing or cheering, sustaining interest during a game, finding ways to improve, channeling aggression into improved functioning, achieving satisfactory self-expression without losing control, and mastering yourself as well as your game. Catch up with the champions on these points and you'll be unbeatable.

Notes

Chapter 1: Choking

1. Frank Deford, "What's With Who's That?" *Sports Illustrated*, April 11, 1977, p. 70.
2. Ted Green, "Do You Know This Man?" *Chicago Daily News*, April 8, 1977, p. 32.
3. Curry Kirkpatrick, "Borg's Hot Hand Took All the Tricks," *Sports Illustrated*, January 31, 1977, p. 16.

Chapter 2: Mind-Body Integration

1. Harry Hopman, *Lobbing into the Sun* (Indianapolis and New York: The Bobbs Merrill Co., Inc., 1975), pp. 78–79.
2. Bill Tilden, *How to Play Better Tennis* (New York: Cornerstone Library, 1951), p. 101.
3. Bridget Byrne, "Ellsworth Vines: The Best of Two Sports Worlds," *Tennis*, September 1978, p. 22.

Chapter 3: Learning Tennis

1. Barry Meadow, "Inside Inner Tennis," *Tennis USA*, April 1977, p. 20.
2. Timothy Gallwey, "You've Got to Increase Your Awareness to Improve Your Play," *Tennis*, March 1977, p. 86.
3. Gladys Heldman, "Inner Needs vs. Sound Ground Strokes," *World Tennis*, April 1977, p. 44.

Chapter 5: Champions

1. Article by Michael Katz, *New York Times*, March 30, 1978.
2. "Jimmy Connors: The Hellion of Tennis," *Time*, April 28, 1975, pp. 47–48.
3. Peter Bodo, "Connors Takes the Winter Wimbledon," *Tennis*, April 1978, p. 136.

4. Dick Stockton, "Jimmy Connors' Backhand," *Tennis USA*, October 1976, p. 47.
5. Gerri Hirshey, "Every Time I Step Out on That Court, I Want to Win," *Tennis USA*, July 1977, p. 19.
6. Ibid.
7. Ibid.
8. Cheryl Bentsen, "Is This 13-Year-Old the Best Female Player Pound for Pound?" *Tennis*, October 1976, p. 51.
9. Ibid.
10. Ibid.
11. Ibid., p. 54.
12. *New York Times*, February 20, 1978.
13. *New York Times*, September 5, 1977.
14. Cheryl Bentsen, *op cit.*
15. Barry Meadow, "I've Learned to Listen to Myself," *Tennis USA*, March 1977, p. 22.
16. Ibid.
17. Article by Gerald Eskenazi, *New York Times*, March 2, 1978.
18. Philip Taubman, "Vilas Tries Harder," *Esquire*, May 9, 1978, p. 47.
19. Spence Conley, "Putting the Stars to Flight," *Tennis USA*, February 1978, p. 27.
20. "Away from the Courts, Ilie Nastase Is Another Man," *Tennis*, May 1978, p. 63.
21. Ibid.
22. Peter Bonventre with Donna Foote, "The Kid Hangs Tough," *Newsweek*, January 29, 1979, p. 83.
23. Robert Cubbedge, "John McEnroe: Confidence Counts," *Tennis*, January 1979, p. 61.
24. Ibid., p. 60.

Index

Here's the book that tells how to start playing tennis just as well as you *think* you can.

Every tennis player experiences the frustration of choking. Under the pressure of winning a point—or a match—your game falls apart and you don't play as well as you *know* you can. Dr. M. Barrie Richmond, a practicing psychiatrist and avid tennis player, goes beyond Gallwey's *Inner Game* by showing you how to integrate body, emotion, and intellect for winning tennis.

Clearly and concisely, Dr. Richmond explains how to identify the psychological blocks that destroy your game and short-circuit coordination, timing, and stamina, leaving you floundering on the court.

Start by confronting and analyzing your feelings about competition and the values you place on winning and losing; then review your frame of mind before (and during) practice sessions and matches, examining reactions to specific shots and lost points. In short, Dr. Richmond puts you in touch with the emotional side of your game, helping you to relax on the court so you can use your skills more effectively. In addition, he evaluates mod-